APT Initiatives Ltd

ESSENTIAL REVISION POCKETBOOK

for AQA A2 Business Studies Students

Unit 3: STRATEGIES FOR SUCCESS

by **Claire Baker**

Consolidating Learning and Simplifying Revision

© **APT Initiatives Limited**, 2009.

Author: **Claire Baker**

All rights reserved. No part of this publication may be reproduced, stored in or introduced into a retrieval system, or transmitted, in any form, or by any means (electronic, mechanical, photocopying, recording or otherwise) without the written permission of APT Initiatives Ltd, or under licence from the Copyright Licensing Agency Limited, of 90 Tottenham Court Road, London W1P 9HE. Any person who does any unauthorised act in relation to this publication may be liable to criminal prosecution and civil claims for damages.

A CIP catalogue record for this book is available from the British Library.

ISBN: 978-0-9556408-6-5

Published by

APT Initiatives Limited
Millstone Lodge
Eaton Upon Tern
Market Drayton
Shropshire
TF9 2BX.

Tel / Fax: 01952 540877
email:sales@apt-initiatives.com
www.apt-initiatives.com

Cover illustration ©iStockphoto.com

Printed and bound by Think Ink, Ipswich, Suffolk, UK.

FOREWORD

This Essential Revision Pocketbook has been produced for students of AQA GCE AS / A Level Business Studies. It covers the essential theory required for the GCE Business Studies specification for AQA A2 Unit 3: Strategies for Success. It contains all the information students need to consolidate their learning and simplify revision.

For each of the core topic areas and individual sub-topic areas listed in the unit specification there are definitions of key terms and concise coverage of the relevant Business Studies theory and concepts. Care has been taken to ensure the information provided is accurate, up-to-date and precise and directly matches the requirements of the unit specification. The pocketbook also provides a highly comprehensive explanation of the skills examiners look for when marking students' answers and how to demonstrate these skills, as well as other essential advice on how to maximise performance in the examination.

The author, Claire Baker, is an experienced teacher, examiner, author and the owner and Managing Director of APT Initiatives Limited. She has taught Business Studies from ages 11 to 19 and has been an examiner, Principal Examiner and Reviser for Business Studies and Business related courses for a leading awarding body.

This Revision Pocketbook is a condensed version of APT Initiatives Ltd's 'Elementary Explanations' written by Claire Baker, which provides in-depth coverage of the essential theory required by the Unit 3 specification.

A range of activities to test and develop students' knowledge and understanding of the Business Studies theory and concepts covered in both these textbooks is provided in other resources available from APT Initiatives Ltd.

APT Initiatives Ltd can be contacted directly with any orders, queries or feedback via the website: www.apt-initiatives.com, via email: support@apt-initiatives.com or by phone: 01952 540877.

CONTENTS

© **APT Initiatives Ltd**, 2009

OPERATIONAL STRATEGIES

HUMAN RESOURCES STRATEGIES

© **APT Initiatives Ltd**, 2009

© **APT Initiatives Ltd**, 2009

© **APT Initiatives Ltd**, 2009

FUNCTIONAL

OBJECTIVES & STRATEGIES

© APT Initiatives Ltd, 2009

USING OBJECTIVES & STRATEGIES

General Introduction to Objectives and Strategies

Objectives: goals or targets that businesses strive to achieve.

Strategies: plans or courses of action required in order to achieve an objective.

The Nature of and Relationship between Objectives & Strategies:

Objectives – *What do we want to achieve?*

Provide direction, focus for decision making, ensure everyone works towards common goal. Should be **SMART** ie **S**pecific, **M**easurable, **A**greed, **R**ealistic & **T**imescaled

↓

Strategy – *How are we going to get there?*

Should be evaluated in terms of: **S**uitability, **A**cceptability, **F**easibility

Determining SMART objectives and the most appropriate strategy requires taking into account:

- Internal capabilities (Strengths + Weaknesses)
- External business environment (Opportunities + Threats)

Functional Objectives and their Relationship with Corporate Objectives

Corporate objectives: goals or targets that concern the business as a whole and provide the boundaries for setting functional eg marketing objectives.

Functional objectives: goals or targets that must be achieved by the individual functional areas into which a business is divided (eg Finance, Marketing, Operations and Human Resources) to ensure that the overall corporate objectives are met.

Corporate Objectives

Eg: *To make a certain %, amount or rate of:*

- sales
- profit
- return (on investment)
- market growth, share

Financial

Eg: *Targets relating to:*

Raising finance
Cash flow / liquidity
Cost minimisation
ROCE
Shareholders' returns

Marketing

Product/brand awareness
Sales
Customer base
Repeat business
Brand / customer loyalty
Market standing (image)
Market share, leadership

Operational

Product / service quality
Production costs
Production volumes
Capacity utilisation
NPD / innovation
Efficiency (including time)
Waste, EVT targets

Human Resource

Recruitment, Labour needs
Training and development
Minimising labour costs
Improving punctuality
Reducing absenteeism
Minimising labour turnover
Employer/ee relations

The Relationship between Functional and Corporate Objectives:

Functional objectives must be achieved by business functions / departments to ensure the overall corporate objectives are met. They must be consistent with, and supportive of, the overall corporate objective(s).

Example:

Corporate objective: **To achieve a 10% increase on profit for the year.**

Functional objectives:

- **Marketing:** To increase sales from £45,000 to £50,000 per month.
- **Human Resources:** To reduce total average unauthorised absence from 10 days to 2 days per month.
- **Finance:** To eliminate bank overdraft by reducing average debtor days from 73 to 56 days within the next 3 months.
- **Production:** To reduce the number of rejects from 2.5% to 1.5% over the next 6 months.

The Relationship between Functional Objectives and Strategies

Corporate strategy: a plan or course of action required to achieve a business's corporate objectives.

Functional strategy: a plan or course of action required to achieve a business's functional objectives.

The Relationship between Functional Objectives and Strategies:

Functional strategies are plans of action required to achieve functional objectives. *Example:*

Marketing Objective	Marketing Strategy
To increase market share from 12 to 20% ie by 8% by 20XX.	Concentrate on middle market sector through product differentiation – a strategy that involves making a firm's product look different from its competitors in the eyes of its customers. It is achieved, for example, through improvements to product packaging, or persuasive TV advertising emphasising product benefits.

© **APT Initiatives Ltd**, 2009

FINANCIAL

STRATEGIES & ACCOUNTS

UNDERSTANDING FINANCIAL OBJECTIVES

Financial Objectives

Financial objectives: goals or targets that must be achieved by the finance function in order to achieve the business's overall corporate objective(s); goals or targets that concern the management of money and other assets.

Examples of Financial Objectives:

Cash Flow / Liquidity

Cash flow: movement of money in / out. Liquidity: cash to meet daily requirements / debts.

Targets might concern:

- the maximum spend per department – budgets.
- reducing customers owing money (debtors).
- reducing inventory (stock) levels.
- increasing / reducing bank overdraft.
- increasing credit granted by suppliers.

Cost Minimisation

Not at the expense of quality – might affect revenues.

An objective and a strategy – essential to achieve:

- profitability, ROCE.
- shareholders' returns.
- market share.

Targets may concern:

- variable costs eg materials, direct labour.
- fixed costs or overheads eg rent, salaries.

ROCE

The amount of operating profit generated from the total capital employed.

$$\frac{\text{Operating Profit}}{\text{Capital Employed}} \times 100$$

Targets may concern:

- increasing Op. profit whilst maintaining same level of capital.
- maintaining Op. profit but reducing amount of capital.

Shareholders' Returns

Potential return on shares:

- Dividends (profit after tax).
- Capital gain.

Targets may concern increasing:

- dividend (or dividend per share, dividend yield).
- share price, market value.

Remember any targets set should be **SMART** and state **by how much** something should be reduced / increased, **by what date** – to enable measurement, aid control.

Internal and External Influences on Financial Objectives

Internal influences: factors stemming from inside the business that can affect decisions over, or success in achieving, financial objectives.

External influences: factors stemming from outside the business that can affect decisions over, or success in achieving, financial objectives.

Internal Influences:

- Corporate objectives.
- Age, Size.
- Legal structure.
- Financial position.
- Worker representation.

External Influences:

- Credit crunch, availability of finance.
- State of economy – business cycle.
- Rates of tax, interest.
- Legislation.
- Competition, State of the market.
- Changes in cost of inputs / materials.

© **APT Initiatives Ltd**, 2009

USING FINANCIAL DATA TO MEASURE AND ASSESS PERFORMANCE

Analysing Balance Sheets

Balance sheet: a snapshot of a firm's worth / financial position at a particular moment in time; shows what the business owns (assets) in monetary terms, and from where funds have been obtained to purchase what it owns (capital and liabilities).

Assets: items owned by the business.

Liabilities: what the business owes to other organisations or individuals.

Capital: money invested or kept within the business by the owners / shareholders.

Accounting Equation: Assets = Capital + Liabilities

Non-current assets (or **fixed assets**): items with a life span of more than a year and do not get used up in the production or provision of a product / service. They can be tangible (eg buildings), intangible (eg trademarks), or financial (eg shares in other businesses).

Depreciation: a cost that occurs when a business writes off the net cost of a fixed asset over its useful life.

Current assets: items usually held for a relatively short period of time, ie under one year such as inventories (stock), trade and other receivables (debtors ie people or other organisations who owe the business money), and cash. They may also include pre-payments ie expenses paid in advance eg insurance.

Current liabilities: monies owed by the business that must be paid within one year from the balance sheet date eg bank overdraft, trade and other payables (creditors ie individuals or businesses to whom the firm owes money). They may also include: dividends payable (percentage of profit to be paid to shareholders), corporation tax (a tax based on company profit), and accruals (creditors who have not yet invoiced the firm eg phone, and wages of those who have worked for the firm but have not yet been paid).

Working capital: the finance available for the day-to-day running of a business; current assets less current liabilities – shown as net current assets on the balance sheet.

Non-current liabilities (**long-term liabilities**): monies owed by a business which do not have to be settled within one year eg loans over 12 months.

Net assets: assets (non-current and current) less liabilities (current and non-current); the part of total assets funded by shareholders' funds or equity (ie capital put into the business by the owners of the business) and not by short-term liabilities or long-term debt; the net value of what the company owns / is worth as a going concern.

Shareholder's equity: money raised by selling shares to family members and friends (Ltd's) or members of the general public (plc's), as well as profit retained within the business (retained earnings) and other funds (reserves) generated from selling shares for more than their nominal value (share premiums), and from selling land or property over the original purchase price (revaluations).

Total equity or **shareholders' funds** (or **capital employed** for a sole trader): the sum of the total amount of money put into the business by owners / shareholders (capital), profit kept within the business (retained earnings), and any other reserves.

Typical Format of a Balance Sheet:

Balance Sheet of ABC plc at 31/3/09

	£	£	£
Non-current Assets (Fixed Assets)			
Premises			1,200,000
Fixtures & Fittings			800,000
Machinery & Equipment			1,900,000
Motor Vehicles			100,000
			4,000,000
Current Assets			
Inventories (Stock)	700,000		
Trade and other Receivables (Debtors)	900,000		
Cash and Cash Equivalents (Cash)	100,000		
		1,700,000	
Current Liabilities			
Bank overdraft	120,000		
Trade and other Payables (Creditors)	880,000		
		1,000,000	
Net Current Liabilities (Net Current Assets)			700,000
Total Assets less Current Liabilities			4,700,000
Non-current Liabilities (Long-term Liabilities)			
Long Term Bank Loan			400,000
Net Assets			**4,300,000**
Shareholders' Equity (Capital and Reserves)			
Ordinary share capital		3,000,000	
Reserves and Retained Earnings (Profit & Reserves)		1,300,000	
Total Equity (Shareholders' Funds)			**4,300,000**

Notes:

Typical format / terms used vary slightly according to legal status.

Since 1 Jan 2005, following EU regulations, plc's financial statements must comply with International Financial Reporting Standards (IFRS). The rule has not yet been extended to Ltd's.

Balance sheet adjacent = typical format for companies in the UK. Terms that may still be used in Ltd's accounts but are no longer used in plc accounts are shown in brackets.

The layout / terminology used in sole trader accounts is similar. The main difference is that there is a 'Capital Account', not a 'Shareholders' Equity', or 'Capital and Reserves' section.

*NB 'No **construction** of accounts or **calculation** of depreciation will be required'.* Thus, students can only be asked to:

- analyse given balance sheet figures, or
- comment on the importance / purpose / effect of working capital or depreciation.

© **APT Initiatives Ltd**, 2009

The Importance of Working Capital:

What is it?

The finance available for day to day running (to meet debts)
Current Assets minus Current Liabilities

Careless attention to working capital = **liquidity problems…**

The Link with Liquidity:

Liquidity = how fast an asset can be converted into cash

most liquid ←→ least liquid

Cash, Shares in other businesses, Debtors, Inventory, Fixed assets

Implications of Poor Liquidity:

Short-term:

- Delaying payments to supplier – poor reputation, refusing future credit.
- Loss in purchasing economies – discounts for bulk purchases.
- Loss of potential business – unable to finance extra expenditure.
- Increased borrowing – increased costs.
- Difficulty borrowing or increased interest rates due to higher risk.

Longer-term:

- Inability to expand / grow – due to lack of finance.
- Creditors asking for business to be declared insolvent – closure.

Managing WC to Secure Liquidity:

- Monitor / control cash – budgets, forecasts.
- Fast production / distribution – faster payment.
- Minimise spending on fixed assets.
- Cut costs.
- Maximise sales and profits.
- Minimise debtors.
- Maximum credit for purchases.
- Reduce inventory / stock levels.

The Importance of Depreciation:

What is it?

A cost that occurs when a business writes off net cost of a fixed asset over its useful life.

net cost =
original cost – expected value at end of life
(historic cost) (residual value)

Why do Assets Depreciate?

- Wear and tear.
- Lack of proper maintenance / servicing.
- Technological advancement.
- Product obsolescence.

Purpose:

- Presenting a true and fair view.
- The matching principle.
- A source of finance / provision for replacement.

Implications:

- Balance Sheet – reduces value of asset each year.
- Income statement – reduces figure for operating profit.
- No effect on cash.

Analysing Income Statements

Income statement (or profit and loss account): a statement showing the net income (or profit) of a business within a trading period ie revenue less all its costs / expenses.

Revenue (turnover): the total value of sales made within a trading period ie year, quarter, month, week, day.

Cost of sales: costs *directly* involved in producing the product or service, eg the cost of materials used to produce a business's product, wages paid to production staff (direct labour).

Gross profit: profit before overheads (other running costs) are deducted; calculated by deducting the cost of sales (direct costs) from revenue (turnover).

Expenses: indirect costs (fixed costs **or overheads),** ie costs *not directly* involved with producing the goods / services, eg wages of office staff, rent, rates, electricity, maintenance and depreciation.

Operating profit (net profit): the surplus / deficit made by a firm's 'normal' activities; calculated by deducting a business's total expenses from the gross profit figure.

Finance income: revenue earned from other activities / interests, eg rent from property owned by the business, interest from cash in bank, dividends from shares held in other companies. On the income statement it is added to the operating profit.

Finance costs: interest payable on any loans. On the income statement it is deducted from the operating profit.

Profit before tax: profit after cost of sales, other expenses and interest have been deducted from sales revenue, but before tax.

Corporation tax: tax levied on the profit of companies, paid as a proportion of profit before tax. It varies according to the size of the profit (before tax) made by the business.

Extraordinary / exceptional items: items unusual to the day-to-day operations of the business eg the sale of assets, the purchase of another business, large bad debts, factory closure and windfall profit on shares held.

Profit for the year (profit after tax): profit for the year after corporation tax has been deducted.

Profit utilisation: how profit is used ie whether the business pays out profit to the owners and, in the case of limited companies, in the form of dividends to shareholders, or whether profit is re-invested in the business.

Profit quality: refers to how sustainable the profit of a particular business is over time.

© **APT Initiatives Ltd**, 2009

Typical Format of an Income Statement:

Income Statement for XYZ plc for the year ending 31/08/09

	£	£
Revenue (Turnover)		1,210,000
Cost of Sales		400,000
Gross Profit		**810,000**
Expenses		
Salaries	400,000	
Advertising	80,000	
Rent	20,000	
Heating & Lighting	16,000	
Telephone	10,000	
Depreciation	14,000	
Total Expenses		540,000
Operating Profit (Net Profit)		**270,000**
Finance Income		-
Finance Costs (Interest)		10,000
Profit before Tax		**260,000**
Taxation		54,600
Profit for the Year (Profit after Tax)		**205,400**

Ltd's traditional Profit & Loss Account format has:

- **'turnover'** instead of 'revenue'.
- **'net profit'** instead of 'operating profit'.
- **'interest** on investments and 'interest paid' instead of 'finance income' or 'finance costs'.
- 'profit **after tax'** instead of 'profit for the year'.
- an **'appropriation section'** – showing dividend payments and retained profit.

The P&L Account of a **sole trader** stops at 'profit before tax'. Drawings are not included. They are deducted from the net profit figure once transferred to the balance sheet:

FINANCED BY:

Opening Capital	20,000
Capital Introduced	10,000
Add Net Profit	25,000
	55,000
less: Drawings	25,000
	30,000

Profit Utilisation:

What is it?

Refers to how the profit is used ie whether the business:

- pays out **dividends** (percentage of after-tax profits paid to shareholders).
- re-invests profit - transferred to '**retained profit**' reserve in balance sheet. May be in the form of cash at bank / in hand, or already spent (eg on stocks, machinery).

Factors that determine PU:

- Age and size of business.
- Access to finance.
- Competition.
- State of the market.
- Rate of inflation.
- Exceptional items.

Profit Quality:

What is it?

Refers to how sustainable the profit of a particular business is. For example, profit may be regarded as lower quality if it stems from the sale of assets or windfall profits on shares - as it is not sustainable.

Significance:

When buying shares, an investor would look at the sustainable earnings. The level of re-investment would also vary according to variation of profit quality.

Using Financial Data for Comparisons, Trend Analysis and Decision Making

Comparisons of financial data: consist of horizontal analysis, vertical analysis, ratio analysis, trend analysis, and industry comparisons.

Horizontal analysis: comparisons between a particular item of financial data for a single business for two or more years. Involves reading *across* the page to compare figures on the same line and - for example - calculating the percentage change (increase or decrease) in operating profit from one year to the next.

Vertical analysis: comparisons between different items on a single financial statement for a single business in any given year. It involves reading *down* the page to compare figures on different lines and calculating component percentages - for example - the percentage gross profit made as a proportion of revenue.

Ratio analysis: compares items listed on a single financial statement (vertical analysis) - for example - current assets in relation to current liabilities, or compares items listed on separate financial statements relating to a business in the same financial year - for example - expressing operating profit as a percentage of total capital (long-term debt and equity) employed.

Trend analysis: the examination of a business's financial data over time to determine whether the business's financial situation is improving or worsening.

Industry comparisons: examining the financial data of a business in relation to similar businesses or industry averages or norms, in order to determine how the business is performing in relation to competitors or similar businesses.

Horizontal Analysis

Examples:

Managers comparing profit from one year to next – to assess success of strategies, or identify the need for change.

Shareholders comparing profit or dividends from one year to next – to determine whether worth continuing to invest, or better to sell shares.

Vertical Analysis

Examples:

Enables potential and existing lenders to assess:

- liquidity / solvency.
- gearing.
- ability to pay interest.

Enables managers to assess how effectively costs are being controlled, by comparing gross or operating profit to revenue (gross / net margin).

Ratio Analysis

Examples:

Analysis of BS and IS figures – *enables…*

…managers to assess:

- return on capital invested (ROCE) .
- asset utilisation (asset turnover).

…shareholders to assess likely return on investment.

Trend Analysis (Inter-year Analysis)

Examples:

Helps shareholders and other potential investors make sound investment decisions – can examine use of profit, trend of dividend payments and assess profit quality.

Useful - for managers - in highlighting potential problems that need to be addressed.

Industry Comparisons

Highlight room for improvement, potential problems / weaknesses.

© APT Initiatives Ltd, 2009

Assessing Strengths and Weaknesses of Financial Data in Judging Performance

Window Dressing: the process of deliberately presenting a better picture of the company than is the case, by 'dressing up' the accounts, some of which are illegal, some of which represent a broad interpretation of accounting rules.

Strengths of Financial Data in Judging Performance:

The Balance Sheet – can be used to assess the:

- net worth - incremental growth (over time). This would indicate the business is a viable concern, and doing well.
- level of gearing. The higher the gearing, the more vulnerable to changes in the external environment, especially interest rates.
- level of liquidity. A greater proportion of current assets to current liabilities indicates ability to meet debts as they fall due.
- level and nature of fixed assets. These can be used as collateral to secure loans to finance growth, or sold off in a crisis to raise cash.

The Income Statement – can be used to assess:

- Growth in turnover. This is a good sign but should be considered in relation to market size (market share).
- Growth in profit. This is a good sign but should be viewed in relation to revenue and capital employed to assess profitability.

Limitations of Financial Data in Judging Performance:

- **Historical** – out of date eg balance sheet 'snapshot' at one moment in time.
- **Missing information – non-financial assets** eg unique selling point, high degree of customer loyalty, highly motivated, highly skilled workforce.
- **Missing information – trading conditions** eg recession, competition.
- **Inflation** eg growth in turnover due to prices rising not sales volume.
- **Personal judgements / estimates** eg re: asset value, bad debts.
- **Different valuation methods** eg for stock, depreciation – makes inter-firm comparisons different.
- **Different accounting periods** – making inter-firm comparisons difficult.
- **Window dressing** – see adjacent.

<u>**Main limitation**</u> – on own shows ***what*** has happened, does not tell you ***why***. Extra information eg trading conditions, inflation, HR needed to fully assess performance.

Window Dressing – *Examples:*

- Falsifying dates of costs and revenue eg delaying payment of invoice, including revenue for work not yet complete / invoiced.
- Brand valuations – highly subjective – boosting intangible fixed assets figure.
- Selling and leasing back assets shortly before balance sheet date to boost liquidity.
- Manipulating figures for working capital items eg stock, debtors, creditors and cash.
- Repaying debt before year end and taking out loan after balance sheet date – to temporarily suppress gearing.

INTERPRETING PUBLISHED ACCOUNTS

Conducting Ratio Analysis

Ratio analysis: compares items listed on a single financial statement (vertical analysis) - for example - current assets in relation to current liabilities; or compares items listed on separate financial statements relating to a business in the same financial year - for example - expressing operating profit as a percentage of total capital (long-term debt and equity) employed.

Liquidity Ratios: *Measure the amount of cash available to meet daily requirements / the ability to meet debts as they fall due.*

If a business has insufficient money to pay its debts, it could be declared insolvent and forced - by creditors - to close to sell off business assets to raise the money required to pay these debts.

- **Current Ratio: Current assets / Current liabilities = X : 1** Accountants' ideal: 1.5 to 2 : 1.
- **Acid Test Ratio: Current assets – inventories (stock) / Current liabilities = X : 1** Accountants' ideal: 1:1.

'Current' means receivable or payable within 12 months. Thus, a ratio of less than 1 to 1 may not mean the business is insolvent. Certain bills eg tax, dividends, may not need to be paid until 6 months time. A firm may also have fixed assets they can sell to raise cash.

Profitability Ratios: *Measure the ability of the business to generate profit.*

Return on Capital Employed (ROCE): Operating profit / Total capital employed (total equity + non-current liabilities) **x 100 = X%**

- A direct measure of the main task of management, which is to maximise the return on capital employed.
- Compare with previous years, similar firms / industry norms, interest earned in bank.
- The higher the percentage, the better the performance.

Can be improved by:

- Increasing operating profit whilst maintaining the same level of capital investment.
- Maintaining operating profit but reducing the amount of capital it takes to generate this amount of profit.

© **APT Initiatives Ltd**, 2009

Financial Efficiency Ratios: *Measure the ability of a firm to use or control the use of its assets.*

Asset Turnover:

- *Measures how many pounds worth of sales a business generates from the assets employed.*
- **Revenue / Net assets = X times.** Compare with previous years or other firms in the same industry.
- Improved by: boosting sales from existing assets eg more effective promotion; selling off under-utilised assets.

Inventory (Stock) Turnover:

- *Measures the number of times in a year a business sells and replenishes its inventory.*
- **Cost of sales / Inventory = X times per year.** The higher the figure the more efficient - reduces obsolescence, stock holding costs.
- **Inventory / Cost of sales x 365 = No of days stock is held.** The lower the figure the more efficient.
- Compare with other firms in the same industry (and previous figures).
- Improved by: reducing the average level of inventory held eg through JIT; increasing the rate of sales without raising stock levels.

Payables' (Credit) Collection period:

- *Measures the number of days it takes a business to pay any money owed to its suppliers (creditors).*
- **Payables (Creditors) / Credit purchases x 365 = No. of days.**
- Ideally should be higher than the receivables (debt) collection period. If shorter, this could lead to a cash flow problem.
- Improved by negotiating extension with suppliers, but this could lead to loss of discount for prompt payment.

Receivables' (Debt) Collection Period:

- *Measures the number of days it takes a business to receive any money owed by its customers (and other debtors).*
- **Receivables (Debtors) / Credit sales x 365 = No. of days.**
- Compare with previous figures rather than similar businesses. Should be kept as low as possible to minimise cash flow problems.
- Improved by: reducing the credit period (but could lose customers to alternative suppliers); offering discounts for prompt payment (but must ensure loss of income does not outweigh benefits eg lower admin costs, discounts from suppliers); improved credit control.

Gearing Ratios: *Measure the extent to which a business is dependent upon borrowed funds.*

- **Non-current (long-term) liabilities / Total capital employed** (total equity + non-current ie long-term liabilities) **x 100 = X%**
- **Total liabilities / Equity plus total liabilities x 100 = X%** or **Long-term debt / Equity x 100 = X%**
- The higher the gearing, the higher the risk as: the business is committed to meeting interest payments, which has a negative effect on cash flow and net profit; loans are often secured on a business's fixed assets and if the business cannot meet interest payments the lender has the right to claim the asset; debtors have priority over owners / shareholders if the business fails.

Shareholder Ratios: *Measure the ability of the business to generate a return to shareholders on their investment.*

Dividend per Share:

- *The amount of money shareholders receive(d) per share.*
- **Total dividends payable or received / Number of shares issued = X pence.**
- Compare with other companies in the same sector and / or previous years.
- Increased by: greater profits; distributing greater proportion of profit as dividends; buying back shares whilst maintaining the dividend.

Dividend Yield:

- *The rate of return a shareholder gets by comparing the market value of the shares with the dividend received.*
- **Dividend paid on ordinary shares / Market price per share x 100 = X%.**
- Compare with other companies in the same sector and / or previous years, and the annual interest that could be received if shares were sold and the money invested in a bank / building society.
- Increased by: a factor lowering the market price per share; distributing a greater proportion of profit as dividends.

Note: The specification states *'candidates will be given a table of relevant formulae for ratios as part of the examination paper where appropriate'*. Thus, students will not be expected to know from memory the formula for calculating specific ratios. They will be expected to: select the correct data from text to calculate ratios; interpret and comment on the result; use calculations to support arguments made.

© **APT Initiatives Ltd**, 2009

Assessing the Value and Limitations of Ratio Analysis in Measuring Performance

Use and Value:

Can answer 3 key questions re: business success, concerning:

- **efficiency of management.**
- **financial stability.**
- **how well the owners / shareholders are doing.**

Meaningful when comparing performance:

- **over time** – to identify trends, whether things improving, worsening, staying the same.
- **with other businesses** – encourages investigation to identify reasons for lower performance and ways to improve performance.
- **accountancy norms**.

For **management** – highlights problems – indicates where action may be required.

For **shareholders** – aids investment decisions.

Limitations: *Any of the following can distort the figures or affect the validity of comparisons:*

1. Changes in the value of money ie **inflation**.
2. Changes in the **accounting methods** used within a business.
3. Changes in **a business's activities** from one year to the next.
4. Changes in the **external business environment** / market and trading conditions.
5. Differences in **product mix, cost structure, objectives and strategies** of business – even those operating within the same industry.
6. Differences in **financial year ends.**
7. Differences in **methods used to value assets** eg to value stock, allow for depreciation.
8. Reliance on **personal judgement** eg estimation of bad debts.
9. The practice of **window dressing** eg by keeping stock levels artificially low, chasing debtors just before the financial year end.
10. **Outdated information** – accounts on which the ratios are based may be several months old.
11. **Missing published financial information** eg sales volume and selling price.
12. **Missing other vital business information** eg quality of product, quality of human resources.

NB: Points 1 to 4 are particularly relevant for comparisons over time, points 5 to 8 are particularly relevant to inter-firm comparisons, and point 5 for comparisons of accounting norms.

Ratios can be useful for assessing performance and highlighting potential weaknesses / problems, but do not provide the answers. Further investigation is required to fully judge performance, and to determine possible causes and potential solutions to problems.

SELECTING FINANCIAL STRATEGIES

Raising Finance

Personal sources of finance: savings in banks or building societies, loans from friends and family, funds from redundancy payments.

Trade credit: an interest free period in which to pay for goods / services received from suppliers - typically between 30 to 70 days.

Overdrafts: arrangements between a firm and its bank or building society to withdraw more money from its bank account than that which is deposited in it, to an agreed limit. Interest is charged on any amounts overdrawn.

Leasing: business rents a fixed asset rather than purchasing it outright. Ownership of the asset remains with the finance company.

Hire purchase: an asset is purchased by putting down a deposit and paying the remainder in instalments over an agreed period of time. The asset is owned once the final instalment has been made.

Sale of assets: the selling of fixed assets owned by the business that are no longer used, or not considered to be making enough contribution to profits.

Retained profit: profit re-invested after all expenses, tax and any dividends to shareholders have been paid.

Loan capital: a business is advanced a set figure and repays the amount over an agreed period of time, at an agreed rate of interest.

Mortgages: loans used to purchase land and buildings and are usually secured on such property.

Debentures: a type of loan where the money to be raised is divided into smaller units (debentures) and members of the public (via the Stock Exchange) are invited to lend money to the business for a fixed period of time (usually long-term) at a fixed rate of interest.

Share capital: finance raised by selling shares in the business - to family and friends in the case of private limited companies, or members of the general public in the case of public limited companies.

Venture capital: finance supplied by merchant banks and specialised commercial banks or venture capital companies, who usually expect to take a minority shareholding in the business for a set period of time.

Government grants: financial assistance from the EU and UK government, for specific regions, purposes, industries and projects.

Short, Medium and Long Term Financial Requirements and Methods:

- **Short** – up to 1 year - for running expenses eg trade credit, overdraft.
- **Medium** – 1 to 5 years - for medium term assets (machinery) eg leasing, medium-term loan.
- **Long-term** – more than 5 years -long-life assets (buildings) eg long-term loan, share capital.

Factors Affecting Choice:

Purpose, Objectives, Preferences of Owners, Legal structure, Financial position, Age, Size, Reputation, Government policy, Interest rates.

© **APT Initiatives Ltd**, 2009

Method	Advantages	Disadvantages
Personal sources	• Often no interest payments (unlike bank loans)	• Owner carries financial risk
Trade credit	• Interest free (unlike overdrafts)	• Loss of discount for prompt payment
Overdrafts	• Simple, quick to arrange, flexible, convenient • Relatively cheap – only charged on outstanding balance	• Expensive used regularly for large amounts • Repayable on demand
Leasing & Hire purchase	• Use of asset without large capital outlay • Flexibility to change equipment, update at little extra cost • Service / maintenance often included • Payments can be offset against tax *Additional advantage of hire purchase:* • Balance sheet position improved once final instalment made	• More expensive in long run than outright purchase
Sale of assets	• No interest payments (unlike loans) • No dilution of ownership and control (unlike shares)	• Need to ensure sale will not restrict future flexibility
Retained profit	• Available immediately – no need to publicise assets or shares for sale, apply for and negotiate loans • No interest payments (unlike loans) • No dilution of ownership and control	• May not be popular with shareholders who would rather receive greater dividends • Sole reliance on profits could mean expansion is slow / limited
Loans	• Relatively simple and quick to arrange, providing satisfactory financial history and collateral (if required), plus sound plans	• Interest – cost, gearing, cash flow • Collateral is often required
Mortgages	• As with loans	• As with loans, *plus* arrangement fee *and…* • Cost of professional valuation of property
Debentures	• No dilution of ownership or control (unlike shares)	• Debenture holders - priority over shareholders • Interest payable even if loss making
Share capital	• No interest payments (unlike loans) • Dividend payments (to ordinary shareholders) are not fixed *NB Success depends on whether perceived to be:* • Soundly managed • Have a good history of dividends • Have sound proposals for investment	• Can be a slow process • Dilutes ownership and control *If converting from ltd to plc…* • Process particularly slow and expensive • Threat of take-over • Greater disclosure requirements
Venture capital	• No interest payments (unlike loans) • Can provide large sums – often £2 million plus • Most offer expert management support	• Can be complex, time consuming process • Legal and accounting fees • Dilution of ownership, control & profits • Many want relatively quick return
Government grant	• Usually lower interest rate than bank loans	• Applying can be costly – certified accounts • Conditions often apply • Non-financial costs eg grants may be publicised

Implementing Profit Centres

Profit centre: a unit within a business that generates revenue and incurs costs and has its own income statement.

Role, Purpose, Benefits: Profit centres aid…

- monitoring and control.
- motivation and performance.
- decision making.

Establishing Profit Centres:

1. Break down products / services into different markets / segments.
2. Record revenue received for each.
3. Allocate direct costs to each.
4. Summarise the 'common' fixed costs and allocate these to each on a rational basis.

Potential Difficulties / Disadvantages of Implementing Profit Centres:

- Co-ordination – harder as the firm is divided into more units.
- Increased pressure on junior managers.
- Interdepartmental conflict and competition - narrow view - need regular communication.
- Actual profit dependent on external factors.
- Not all revenues or costs can be directly associated with particular part of business.

Methods of allocating costs:

Full costing:

All indirect costs incurred by a business are **totalled** then divided and allocated to cost centres according to one criterion eg according to output by volume or value.

Advantages	Disadvantages
• Simple, inexpensive. • If used to set price ensures costs covered.	• Inaccurate - can be misleading - lead to poor decisions.

Absorption costing:

Each overhead is absorbed **separately** by the profit centre according to logical criteria eg rent and rates allocated according to floor space taken up by the centre.

Advantages	Disadvantages
• Fair. • More accurate.	• Some workers may be multi-skilled and used by more than one centre; there may be some common floor area. • More time consuming and expensive to apply.

Marginal or contribution costing:

Direct costs **only** are allocated to the profit centre. Indirect costs are only included when preparing the whole firm's profit and loss account.

Advantages	Disadvantages
• Simple. • Allows direct comparison. • Focuses attention on products making only a small contribution.	• Misleading – cost centre may generate high proportion of overheads yet be seen as making positive contribution to profit. • If used to set prices, need to be careful to cover total fixed costs.

© APT Initiatives Ltd, 2009

Cost Minimisation

Cost minimisation: involves identifying all the costs involved in producing a business's product or service and investigating whether any of these costs can be reduced without affecting sales or the quality of the product or service provided.

A Means to Achieve Financial and Corporate Objectives:

- Can help maximise profit and return on investment.
- Can help increase market share - enables the business to be more competitive on price.
- *However*, cost cutting strategies may impact on other functional areas - impact needs to be carefully considered - close liaison with other functions required.

Minimising Wages & Salaries – *Eg's:*

- Review / cut hours where possible
- Flexible working - temporary vs overtime
- Training - productivity
- Outsourcing
- Automation

Minimising Travel Expenses – *Eg's:*

- Research / fill at cheapest station
- Vehicle maintenance
- Avoid rush hour travel
- SatNav systems
- Book flight, train in advance
- Negotiate better deals - cars, hotels
- Use pool system for vehicles
- Smaller, more fuel efficient vehicles

Minimising Rent, Leasing – *Eg's:*

- Renegotiate rate - for longer lease?
- Review / cut floor space, sublet
- Use homeworking / teleworking
- Relocate some or all the business

Minimising Energy – *Eg's:*

- Better deals from alternative suppliers
- Shift work - off-peak tariffs
- Turn off lights, equipment not in use
- Close doors, windows, seal cracks
- Reduce thermostat 1 or 2 degrees
- Insulate rooms, hot water tank, pipes
- Energy saving bulbs
- Bulk purchase of fuel at off-peak times
- Programmable thermostats
- Well maintained equipment
- More energy efficient equipment
- Alternative source eg sun, wind, water

Minimising Water Rates / Bills – *Eg's:*

- Insulating pipes against frost
- Maintenance of water-using equipment
- Staff check, report, fast repair of leaks
- Re-use of process water
- Alternative source eg rain, grey water
- Water-minimising controls
- Water-efficient equipment

Minimising Material Costs – *Eg's:*

- Compare / renegotiate prices
- Alternative, cheaper, reliable suppliers
- More bulk purchases - discounts
- Reducing stock levels
- Using newer lower cost materials
- Improving staff ability / motivation
- Planned, preventative maintenance

Minimising Business Rates – *Eg's:*
By moving to a…

- smaller premises
- different area where rates are lower

Telephone – *Eg's:*

- Better rates / tariffs - shop around
- Phone calls through Internet - VoIP

Promotion – *Eg's:*

- Shop around for best rates
- Promotion via email or with orders

Printing, Postage, Stationery – *Eg's:*

- Correspond with customer via email
- As with material costs

Repairs & Maintenance – *Eg:*

- Planned, preventative maintenance

Legal and Professional Fees – *Eg:*

- Shop around for best rates

Bank Charges, Interest – *Eg:*

- Shop around for cheapest credit

Allocating Capital Expenditure

Capital Expenditure: spending on the acquisition, modification or improvement of a physical asset that is likely to last more than a year eg building, vehicle. Includes installation and legal costs. Does not include maintenance costs.

Revenue Expenditure: spending on items used up on the day to day running and management of the business eg payment for materials, labour, energy and repairs.

Difference between Capital and Revenue Expenditure – *Examples:*

	Capital Expenditure	Revenue Expenditure
Buildings	• Cost of the building • Cost of extension, modification, improvement • Legal fees eg to obtain planning • Architect fees • Utility installation costs	• Maintenance • Repairs
Vehicles	• Cost of the vehicle • Cost of any alterations to fix prior problems (if second hand) or improve performance	• Road Tax, MOT • Insurance • Fuel • Servicing and repairs
Machinery	• Cost of the machinery • Cost of any alterations to fix prior problems (if second hand) or improve performance • Installation cost, Training cost • Cost of modifications / upgrades	• Insurance • Maintenance / Servicing • Repairs

The Key Differentiator:

If the expenditure simply **maintains** the asset in its current condition, then it is an item of revenue expenditure as opposed to capital expenditure. In which case, the total cost should be deducted fully in the year it occurred and recorded on the income statement as a cost against revenue.

Allocating Capital Expenditure:

The total expense is:

- a cash outflow on the cash flow statement.
- a non-current asset on the balance sheet.
- **not** shown on the income statement.
- **Capitalised** - cost is spread over asset's useful life - the asset is **depreciated.**

Depreciation affects **both** the balance sheet and income statement figures. *Example:*

Machinery costs: £1 million.
Estimated life: 10 years. Residual Value: £0.
Annual allowance for depreciation: £100,000.

End of Year 1:
Net Book Value on BS = £900,000.
Depreciation charge on IS = £100,000.

End of Year 2:
Net Book Value on BS = £800,000.
Depreciation charge on IS = £100,000.

...and so on

© **APT Initiatives Ltd**, 2009

MAKING INVESTMENT DECISIONS

Why Businesses Invest – Helping to Reach Functional Objectives

Investment: concerns spending money now in the hope of reaping greater reward in relation to the original investment in the future.

Types of Investment:

- Capital goods eg land, buildings, vehicles and machinery.
- Purchase of another business, eg competitor, supplier.
- Investment in R&D.
- Investment in promotion.
- Investment in NPD.
- Investment in training.

Why Businesses Invest:

To: reap greater reward in the future; fulfil functional objectives *eg investment in…*

- capital goods / another business – to achieve growth in sales or market share.
- new machinery – to fulfil operational target re: volumes, quality, costs, environment.
- a supplier business – to minimise costs, maximise shareholder returns.
- R&D – to achieve operational targets re: new product development.
- a promotional campaign – to achieve targets re: sales, market standing/share, liquidity.
- training – to make full use of workforce potential; to meet targets re: health & safety.

Conducting Quantitative Investment Appraisal

Investment appraisal: considers the benefits of an investment decision in relation to the anticipated costs. Benefits might include increased revenues and / or reduced costs. Costs might include the initial capital outlay and running costs.

Payback: the amount of time it takes for an investment to recover or pay back the initial cost of the investment (capital outlay).

Average rate of return: measures the (average) net return each year (profit or savings) generated from the investment as a percentage of the initial capital cost of the investment.

Net present value: calculates and then totals the present values of all the expected future cash flows of an investment (using discounting factors based on a pre-determined interest rate to arrive at the 'present values'), and subtracts these from the original cost of the investment.

Payback: Annual net cash flow / Initial capital outlay. *Example:*

	Project A (£)	Project B (£)	Project C (£)
Initial Investment	100,000	100,000	100,000
*Cash Flow			
End of Year 1	30,000	10,000	60,000
End of Year 2	30,000	15,000	40,000
End of Year 3	30,000	25,000	25,000
End of Year 4	30,000	40,000	15,000
End of Year 5	30,000	60,000	10,000
Total Cash Flow	150,000	150,000	150,000

*Cash flow = revenue – operating costs or net savings (not initial investment).

Project C: all £60k from Yr 1 + all £40k from Yr 2 = **2 years exactly.**
Project B: Yrs 1 to 4 = £90k, plus £10k / £60k (of Yr5) x 12 = **4 yrs 2 months.**
Project A: Yrs 1 to 3 = £90k, plus £10k / £30k (of Yr4) x 12 = **3 yrs 4 months.**

Project C has the shortest payback = least **risk.**

Average Rate of Return (ARR):

Average Annual net return / Initial capital outlay X 100. *Example:*

Capital outlay £45,000. Project has 4 year life. Net cash flow end of: Yr 1 is £10,000, Yr 2 is £15,000, Yr 3 is £20,000, Yr 4 is £20,000.

Steps - calculate:

1. Total net cash flow over life of project = £65,000.
2. Net return over life: total net cash flow – capital outlay = £20,000.
3. Average annual net return: net return / no. of yrs (expected life) = £5,000.
4. ARR%: average annual net return / initial capital outlay = **11.11%.**

For every £1 invested, the project generates just over 11p.

Net Present Value (NPV): *Example:*

Project Z cash flows: Yr 0 = (£50,000), Yr 1 = £20,000, Yr 2 = £30,000, Yr 3 = £15,000

How much must be invested now to get £20k in a yr, at current interest rates? Assume 5% interest rate.

£q x 1.05 = £20,000
£q = £20,000 / 1.05
£q = **£19,048** (rounded up)

How much must be invested now to get £30k in 2 yrs? NB assume 5% interest rate.

£q x 1.05^2 = £30,000
£q x 1.1025 = £30,000
£q = £30,000 / 1.1025
£q = **£27,211** (rounded up)

How much to get £15k in 3 yrs, with 5% rate?

£q x 1.05^3 = £15,000
£q = £15,000 / 1.157625
£q = **£12,958** (rounded up)

Factors 1 / 1.05, 1 / 1.05^2 etc **<u>are provided</u> in exam**

Total discounted cash flows:	**£59,217**
Deduct original cost:	(£50,000)
To give **NPV:**	**£9,217**

If **positive** (as above) **accept.** If negative – reject.

Note: Accuracy dependent on accuracy of data used in cash flow forecasts and discount figures. Need to carefully select/check source + quality of data used.

© **APT Initiatives Ltd**, 2009

Investment Criteria

Investment criteria: pre-determined conditions laid down by key decision makers within the business that potential investments must meet - for example - a certain percentage return, within a certain timeframe.

Financial Criteria – *Examples:*

- Maximum capital outlay.
- Minimum payback period.
- Minimum ARR% - higher than interest rate.
- A positive Net Present Value (NPV).

Non-financial Criteria – *Examples:*

- Comply with legislation.
- Match industry standards.
- Improve reputation / relations with staff, customers, suppliers, community, etc.
- Strengthen / protect the business against rivals / threats.

Assessing the Risks and Uncertainties of Investment Decisions

Risks associated with investment decisions: the chance the hoped for or expected outcome is not achieved. It exists where the exact outcome of a particular action or event is unknown, but the possible outcomes and their individual likelihood of occurrence <u>are</u> known.

Uncertainty over investment decisions: exists where the likelihood of occurrence of certain events are unknown.

Why is there Uncertainty?

External uncontrollable factors – *eg…*

- New competitor – affect forecast cash inflows.
- Interest rates – affect forecasts for cash inflows and outflows.

Assessing Risk & Uncertainty:

Involves asking the following:

1. What is the expected return?
2. What are the possible outcomes?
3. Will any threaten firm's survival?
4. Can the risk be reduced?
5. What is the reward in relation to the risk?

Managing Risk & Uncertainty:

- **Sensitivity Analysis:** identify assumptions behind forecast outcomes, test how outcome alters if assumptions vary.
- **Decision Trees:** diagrams with alternatives relating to possible problem + all possible outcomes stemming from alternatives, with the likelihood of the different outcomes occurring, and the associated financial consequences.
- **Setting higher targets** re: payback, ARR or higher discount rates for NPV.

Evaluating Quantitative and Qualitative Influences in Investment Decisions

Quantitative influences: factors that can easily be measured eg size, weight, amount of something. In the context of an investment this might, for example, concern the forecast net financial return and the length of time it takes to pay back the initial cost of the investment.

Qualitative influences: factors that cannot easily be measured eg thoughts, feelings and outcomes in terms of human relations, accomplishments and skills. In the context of an investment this might, for example, concern the potential impact on staff morale.

Example – *New Machinery:*

Quantitative Factors	
Costs	**Benefits**
• Initial capital and installation costs. • Training costs. • Cost of any redundancies. • Running and maintenance costs. • Cost of any financing – interest.	• Reduction in running (including staffing) and maintenance costs. • Reduction in costs of reworking / disposals due to improved quality. • Increased profits as a result of the above.
Qualitative Factors	
Costs	**Benefits**
• Poor staff relations and fall in reputation as an employer as a result of redundancies.	• Improved morale and fewer accidents (which could be quantified) due to better safety of use.

Evaluation of Payback

Pros:
- Simple to understand.
- Easy to calculate.
- Useful initial screening.
- Emphasis on early return.
- Useful measurement of risk.
- Useful if liquidity important.
- Useful where product has short life span.

Cons:
- Ignores timing of payments.
- Ignores cash after payback – profitability.
- Short-term view.
- Ignores inflation and opportunity cost.
- Not consider alternative of money in bank.

Evaluation of ARR

Pros:
- Simple to understand.
- Relatively easy to calculate.
- Uses yield in all years.
- Quick estimate of profitability.
- Can compare with interest rate.

Cons:
- Timing of return ignored.
- Calculates av. profits - may vary.
- Ignores inflation, opportunity cost

Evaluation of NPV

Pros:
- Takes into account amount and timing of all cash flows.
- Takes into account time value of money - opp. cost of money in bank.
- Can adjust discount factor for risk.

Cons:
- More complex and time consuming.
- Assumes opportunity cost remains the same throughout the project.

Overall Evaluation of Quantitative Methods

Valuable aid to decision making - force managers to investigate cash flows, consider options, outcomes, consequences. *However,* difficult to estimate cash flows - only as good as estimates upon which based.

Qualitative Influences

Business objectives.

Corporate image.

Employee-employer relations

Attitude to risk.

© **APT Initiatives Ltd**, 2009

MARKETING STRATEGIES

UNDERSTANDING MARKETING OBJECTIVES

Marketing Objectives

Marketing objectives: goals or targets that must be achieved by the marketing function (department) within a business to ensure the business's corporate objectives are achieved.

Product / Brand Awareness

Important:

- at start-up.
- to launch a new product.
- to sell more to the same market.
- to break into a new market.

Involves:

- investment in promotion.

Sales, Customer Base

Most common. Likely to involve:

- **promotion** - to raise awareness.
- **incentive** - encourage purchase.

Market Share

$$\frac{\text{ABC's sales value or volume}}{\text{Total sales of whole market}} \times 100$$

Common in competitive markets.

Ways to increase:

- improve quality / benefits.
- reduce selling price.
- special offers.
- more effective promotion.

Repeat Business, Brand / Customer Loyalty

Important when:

- product needs replacing / renewing in immediate, short, medium term.

Eg includes:

- supermarkets, insurance brokers, cars.

Might involve:

- improving product / service quality.
- special offers, bonus - repeat purchase.
- regular communication.

Market Standing / Position (Image)

Concerned with:

- creating a distinct image.
- changing perceptions.

Important when a business:

- faces significant competition.
- wants to target a new segment.
- wants target market to buy for first time.

Involves:

- researching perceptions, promotion to change / reinforce perceptions.

Role and Purpose: *Provide a…*

- focus for decision making - marketing strategy.
- common goal - aids motivation.
- means to measure performance - aids control.

SMART Marketing Objectives:

Like all objectives they should be:

Specific, **M**easurable, **A**greed (by key individuals concerned), **R**ealistic (taking into account SWOT), **T**imescaled. *Eg:* increase awareness of product X by 25% within the year.

The Link with Corporate Objectives:

Example – New business:

- Corporate: survival, breakeven.
- Marketing: recognition, customer base.

Example – Established business:

- Corporate: sales growth, expansion.
- Marketing: brand loyalty, market share, new products / markets.

© **APT Initiatives Ltd**, 2009

Assessing Internal and External Influences on Marketing Objectives

Internal influences on marketing objectives: factors stemming from inside the business that can affect decisions over, or success in achieving, marketing objectives.

External influences on marketing objectives: factors stemming from outside the business that can affect decisions over, or success in achieving, marketing objectives.

Internal Influences – *Examples:*

- Corporate objectives.
- Finance available.
- Size, ability, motivation of workforce.
- Productive capacity.
- Production methods.

External Influences – *Examples:*

- Political eg privatisation, tax policy.
- Legal.
- Economic eg interest rates, employment.
- Social eg demography, attitudes.
- Technology - new markets, machines.
- Competitor activities.
- Cost of inputs, quality of suppliers.

ANALYSING MARKETS AND MARKETING

Reasons For, and the Value of, Market Analysis

Market analysis: a process that attempts to identify and measure market characteristics through a range of market research techniques in order to inform decision making and planning. It may, for example, include identifying and measuring market size, segments, growth, share, level and intensity of competition, and distribution channels.

Reasons:

- **Descriptive** - What is happening now?
- **Predictive** - What is likely to happen?
- **Explanatory** - Why is it happening?
- **Exploratory** - Investigate new products / strategies.

Overall…

- Identifies, tests, measures business opportunities and potential in a market.
- Generates vital info to aid decision making and planning.

Value:

Minimises risk of failure – more likely to detect potential problems / weaknesses in decisions / strategies – saving the:

- cost of the initial investment.
- business's long-term reputation.

Increasingly important, due to:

- the rapid pace of change.
- increased competition.
- better educated, more sophisticated consumers.

Methods of Analysing Trends

Sales forecasting: attempts to predict the future behaviour of sales.

Sales forecast: a prediction of the sales (in terms of volume or value) that will be achieved in a given period of time.

Trend: the general pattern or underlying movement of the data being examined.

Moving averages (or rolling averages): a collection of averages calculated for a group of data shown over a certain number of (usually) equal time periods.

Extrapolation: the use of past data to establish trends (ie the general direction in which the data is moving), which are then projected forward into the future.

Correlation: the relationship between two variables eg the weather and sales of ice creams.

Test marketing: involves the launch of a product on a limited scale in a representative part of the market to assess consumer reaction and forecast future sales.

Test markets: segments within a market (eg a geographical area or demographic group) considered to be representative of the market as a whole. They are chosen to trial a new product or service in order to assess the likelihood of its success within the whole market, and identify potential problems / weaknesses and allow them to be rectified prior to a full launch.

Role & Value of Sales Forecasting:

Vital role in marketing, production, financial and HR planning – can help plan:

- **use of resources** - enables other variables to be forecasted eg material purchases, labour, cash flow.
- **price changes** - if forecasted sales do not allow objectives to be met.
- **capacity increase** - if current capacity is insufficient to meet forecasts / targets.

Overview of Methods:

Quantitative – analysis of numerical data. **Qualitative** – opinions, experience. Businesses often use both. AQA Unit 3 – emphasis on **quantitative.**

Establishing and Extrapolating Trends through Moving Averages:

Trend: The general pattern / underlying movement of the data.

Value of establishing the trend:

Aids decision making, planning eg market growing or falling, consider:

- increasing / reducing capacity?
- moving into a different market?
- greater emphasis on marketing?

© APT Initiatives Ltd, 2009

Establishing the Trend: Involves calculating moving averages:

1. Select a number of time periods for calculating the average (on a rational basis).
2. Total 1st set of values up to time period selected & calculate average eg Qtr 1+2+3+4 divided by 4.
3. Repeat the process for the set of data, eg Yr 1 Qtr 2+3+4+ Yr 2 Qtr 1, and so on.

Example: Sales rise and fall every 5 yrs. *Thus,* averages calculated using 5 sets of data…

Time (year)	Point in cycle of data	Data: Sales (units)	5 point mov av (Trend)*	Variation (Data – trend)
1	1	350		
2	2	370		
3	3	395	370	25
4	4	375	377	-2
5	5	360	383	-23
6	1	385	386	-1
7	2	400	390	10
8	3	410	396	14
9	4	395	400	-5
10	5	390	402	-12
11	1	405		
12	2	410		
13	3	?		

* Trend is inserted in middle of the points of data, eg first average for yr 1 to yr 5 inserted opposite year 3.

The moving averages can be plotted on a chart and the trend identified…

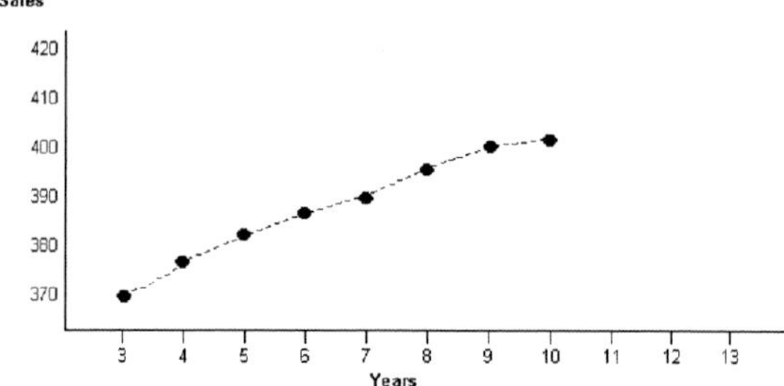

The trend is clearly upward, but there is a flattening off of the data. The trend can then be extrapolated ie projected forward into the future to forecast sales…

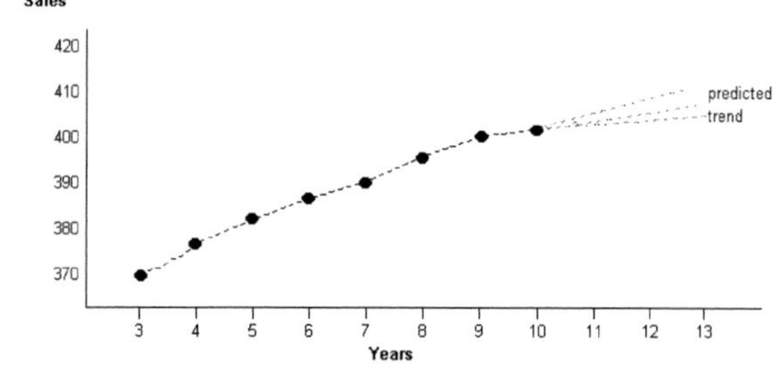

Use and Limitations of Moving Averages and Extrapolation:

- Calculating moving averages and establishing the trend is useful in exemplifying *what* is happening, but it does not explain *why*.
- Making predictions about sales through extrapolation, allows a business to plan. However, it assumes history is repeated, yet factors affecting markets may change eg new competition, war. It should only be used where trading conditions are relatively stable.
- The further into the future a firm tries to predict, the less accurate the prediction.

Correlation:

The strength of the relationship between two variables, eg the relationship between:

- the weather and items of food, clothing.
- expenditure on promotion and sales.
- pay rates and productivity.
- complimentary goods / services.
- substitute goods / services.

Establishing a relationship between variables might assist with the prediction of sales and decisions over marketing strategy.

Graphical Use of Correlation – Scatter Graphs:

Plotting sales of one variable against another.

Independent variable = X (horizontal) axis eg changes in weather.

Dependent variable = Y (vertical) axis eg ice cream

Analysing the results:

- Closely related, move upwards in same direction = **high positive correlation.**
- Sales of one rises, sales of another falls = **negative correlation.**
- Little connection = **weak / low correlation.**
- No relationship = **zero correlation.**

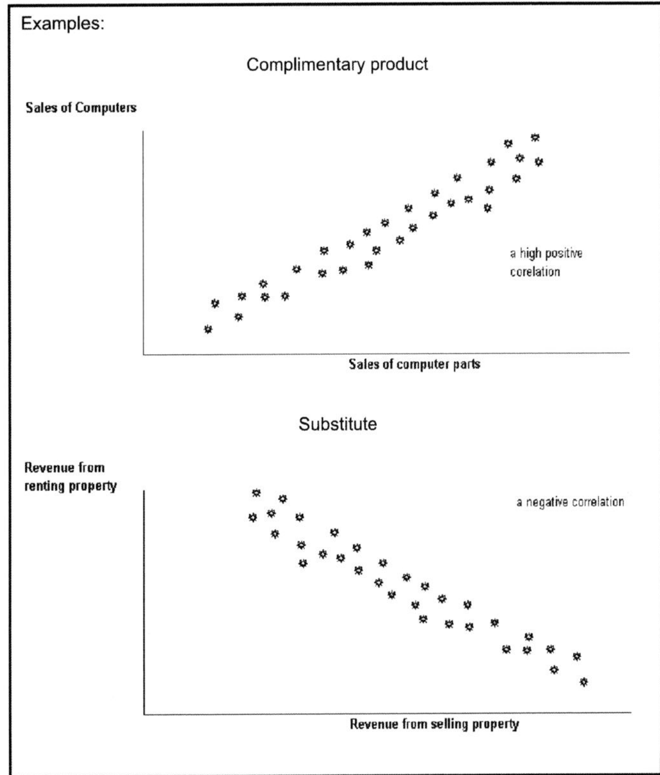

© **APT Initiatives Ltd**, 2009

Lines of Best Fit:

May be able to anticipate future sales by extrapolating the line of best fit between the 2 variables…

Mean for each variable's data is calculated and each pair of values plotted on a diagram (adjacent). A straight line is drawn through the plot so all other plots are on, or close to the line and roughly the same number of plots are above and below.

The closer to the line the plots are, the stronger the correlation.

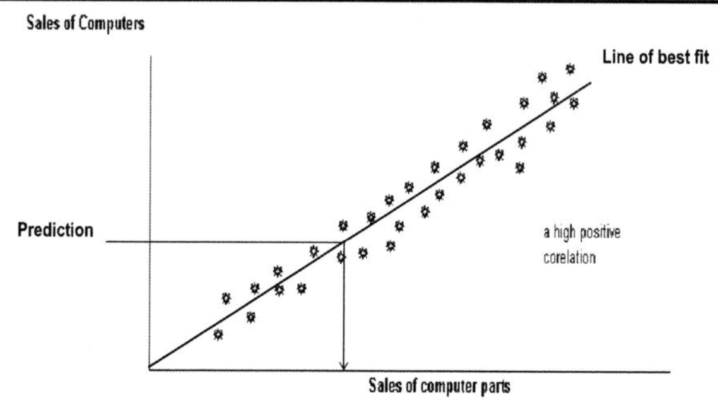

Process of Test Marketing and Review:

Involves launching product on limited scale in representative part of the market to assess customer reaction and forecast future sales. After the test market, the firm will consider:

1. Will it meet a defined **customer need**?
2. What **segment(s)** will it serve?
3. What **position** is it likely to occupy?
4. Does it fit in with overall **objectives**?
5. Will it improve or diminish the firm's **image?**
6. What are the functional **implications**?
7. Do we have the **resources**?
8. If not, can they be **obtained**? At what **cost**?
9. Are the **contribution** possibilities worthwhile?
10. What will be the overall effect on the **financial position**?
11. Are there any **legal aspects** to consider?
12. When is the best **time** to launch?
13. Can the firm **keep to schedule**?

Benefits and Limitations: It can help to determine whether a new product is likely to achieve the desired results. It incurs costs and may not reflect the whole market, but it can save costs in the long run – helping to improve the product before a national launch to ensure people buy it.

Limitations of Correlation and Scatter Graphs:

Many factors affect a particular variable eg investment in advertising may show a positive correlation with sales of a product. But sales may have increased as result of a fall in interest or taxation rates, or closure of a major competitor, for example. Thus, decisions based on judgements about relationships between variables **should not be made** until **all other factors have been taken into account.**

Qualitative Techniques: Based on opinions and experience.

Used when numerical data is scarce; market changes quickly. *Include:*

- Personal insight.
- Historical analysis.
- Market surveys.
- Panel consensus.
- Delphi Technique.

The Use of Information Technology in Analysing Markets

Information technology: The acquisition, processing, storage and dissemination of vocal, pictorial, textual and numerical information by a micro-electronics-based combination of computing and telecommunications (Department of Employment Information Technology). In simple terms it concerns the application of technology to information.

Data Collection:

Increased efficiency eg **mobile phone or internet technology** - can send / receive text, speech, numerical data, pictures, diagrams, at great speed.

Data Presentation:

Most **spreadsheets** have graphical packages - produce diagrams, charts, graphs automatically to suit different needs - increase accuracy, speed with which diagrams are produced and market data can be analysed.

Data Processing and Analysis:

Computers: speed up data processing and allow the study of complex inter-relationships, faster identification of segments and development of marketing strategies to target these segments.

Spreadsheets: perform calculations and allow figures to be manipulated quickly and easily to produce forecasts.

Databases: store customer information and have a file searching, sorting and calculating facility that enables specific information to be quickly and easily retrieved, and data to be rapidly reorganised for specific purposes eg arranging customers in ascending order of sales, as well as the rapid production of letterheads and mailing lists.

Difficulties in Analysing Marketing Data

Limitations of Secondary Data:

- might not be up-to-date – might not represent what is currently happening.
- might not be specific to the business's needs – might not reflect the target market.

Difficulty Securing Resources: Primary data - time consuming, costly - requires finance, skilled staff.

Lack of finance may limit scope of research, sample size and, thus, reduce confidence in the results.

Lack of skilled personnel can lead to:

- invalid data.
- inaccurate calculations.
- incorrect interpretation.

External Factors: Affect the accuracy of the data collated and forecast results, eg changes in:

- competitor activities.
- macro-economic factors.

Thus, even when the data obtained is up-to-date, specific, correctly analysed and interpreted, there is no guarantee it will represent the future.

© **APT Initiatives Ltd**, 2009

SELECTING MARKETING STRATEGIES

Porter's Generic Strategies: Low Cost versus Differentiation

Competitive advantage (CA): something that places an organisation above its rivals, for example, the ability to offer lower prices or a faster, more reliable service. Porter identified 3 strategies through which CA can be achieved: cost leadership, differentiation, focus.

Cost leadership strategy: involves producing at the lowest possible cost, often in order to offer its product or service to customers at the lowest possible price.

Differentiation strategy: involves making the product or service look distinctively different to those of competitors in the eyes of the customers, and in ways valued by customers.

Unique selling point or proposition (USP): a key characteristic of the product or service that differentiates it from similar products or services in the market place.

Focus (or **market segmentation**) strategy: involves focusing on a small part of the overall market and succeeding through, either, cost leadership or differentiation within that small sector of the overall market.

Low Cost – Cost Leadership:

What Does it involve?

Often involves producing / selling large volumes of standard 'no frills' product / service - benefit from economies of scale. The emphasis is on minimising costs eg through:

- new technology, production methods.
- relocating some or all of the business.
- outsourcing non-core / critical activities.
- forwards or backwards vertical integration.
- raising productivity, capital utilisation.

Businesses tend to:

- be **streamlined -** with few hierarchical layers.
- encourage **responsibility / accountability** - cost centres.
- implement **tight cost control** eg budgets, supervision.
- use **incentives** based on cost targets.

When is it appropriate? *Most appropriate when:*

- there is significant price competition.
- the firm sells a standard, homogenous product available from rivals.
- customers are price sensitive or have significant purchasing power.

Advantages:

Enables a business to:

- gain sales, market share, *or…*
- achieve above average profit, *plus…*
- deter new entrants.
- force out a new entrant.
- defend against substitutes.
- cope with pressure to reduce prices.
- more easily absorb increase in costs.
- cope better in a recession.

Disadvantage:

Customers may perceive the business's product / service to be lower quality than other products / services in the marketplace.

Differentiation:

What Does it involve?

Making the product / service stand out might involve:

a) **actual (physical) advantages** eg:
- design - better performance, look.
- additional features.
- better quality materials.
- better packaging.
- easier access.
- faster, more reliable delivery.
- after sales services.

b) **perceived (psychological) advantages** eg through branding and advertising.

Successful differentiation requires:

- thorough awareness and appreciation of the target market and what they value.
- in-depth knowledge of competitor products / services.
- innovation and flexible organisation.

Thus, requires investment in: R&D, new technology, training.

When is it appropriate? *When:*

- there is significant competition.
- firm does not sell a standard, homogenous product - there is scope for differentiation.
- customers are **not** price sensitive.

Advantages:

Allows a higher price, thus greater profits; or attracts more custom – sales, market share.

Can help **build customer loyalty** which can:

- keep customers away from rivals.
- reduce the threat of substitutes.
- deter new entrants.

Few, if any, **close substitutes**, therefore…

- reduces power of big customers re: price.
- enables the firm to pass on cost increases to customers and maintain profitability.

Disadvantages:

Finding ways that are difficult for competitors to imitate can be difficult and costly.

Customers are increasingly sophisticated and tastes can easily and frequently change. This necessitates ongoing investment to identify and develop new ways to stand out in ways that customers value.

Focus:

Advantages:

Provides a better understanding of customers and their needs, thus, more efficient allocation of resources and rapid response to change.

Focus differentiation - helps secure customer loyalty, gain leadership in a particular segment and maximise profits. NB High customer loyalty discourages new entrants and protects against substitutes. **FD** also reduces the power of large firms as there are generally few alternatives

Disadvantages:

In general, lower volumes, *thus*… lower sales, profits *plus*… less power with suppliers. *However,* with focus-differentiation the firm is more able to pass on a cost rise (supplier, other) as customers are less price-sensitive.

As with any strategy, there is the risk of imitation. The market & environment are also constantly changing, affecting the make-up of segments, and requiring changes in strategy.

© **APT Initiatives Ltd**, 2009

Ansoff's Matrix (& Other) Marketing Strategies

Market penetration: increasing sales of present products to present markets.
Market development: increasing sales of present products by selling to new markets.
Product development: involves selling new products to present markets.
Diversification: involves selling new products to new markets.

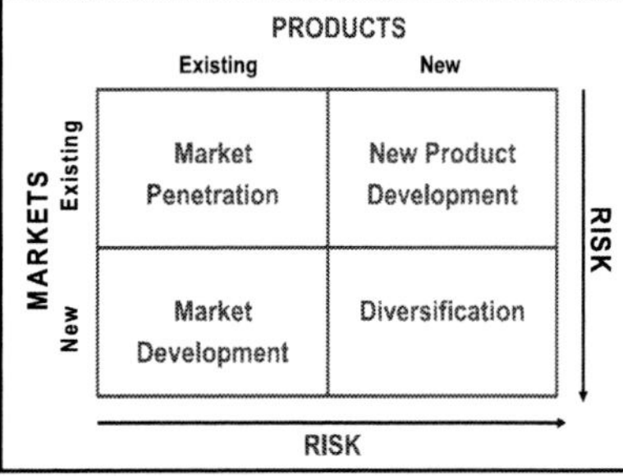

Market Penetration:

Least risky. Only possible if the market is growing, or the firm has competitive advantage to gain share from rivals.

Achieved by: increasing the frequency or quantity purchased amongst existing customers, or attracting users of competitors' brands.

Requires: sound knowledge of customer buying habits and competitor activities; research into the opinions of non-users

Emphasis: often on promotion eg of present product benefits / uses and new product uses.

Product Development:

Can be costly, risky. However, does **not** mean **brand new** - could simply involve:

- changing material, ingredients, colour.
- adding a new feature.
- introducing a new size.
- improving functional performance.

Market Development:

Assumes there are new markets that can be exploited profitably. **More risky** than penetration - involves one unknown, requires more research.

Achieved by: targeting new segments in the same geographical markets, or new geographical markets - difficult if strong cultural differences exist.

Emphasis: often on promotion - careful advertising to effectively position the product in the new market place.

The Right Strategy?

- Depends upon the situation, objectives, resources; takes into account internal and external factors.
- Builds on strengths, explores opportunities.
- Is realistic (resources) and agreed.

Eg: Plenty of opportunity in current market - market penetration. Fierce competition - consolidate or diversify. Strong in R&D - confidence with NPD.

Diversification:

The **most risky.** Often requires considerable research and investment. *But,* can **spread risk** as the firm is less vulnerable to changes in one market. Often adopted when the market is saturated, intense competition, or falling sales - other factors eg recession.

Two types: **Related** – link to present markets and products eg biscuit manufacturer into cereals. **Unrelated** – different industry eg biscuit manufacturer into financial services. The more unrelated, the higher the cost, risk.

Other Strategies:

- Withdrawal / Retrenchment.
- Consolidation.
- Do nothing – maintain existing operations, products and markets.

Methods, Risks and Benefits of Entering International Markets

Direct exporting: where a firm keeps production in the home country but independently researches and selects a foreign wholesaler or retailer to sell its products to a foreign end-customer, or independently researches and sells it products direct to a foreign end-customer.

Indirect exporting: where a firm keeps production in the home country but sells its products to a foreign market through an intermediary in the home country, or a foreign agent.

Licensing: where a business obtains a licence to sell another business's product in exchange for a fee.

Franchising: where a business gives another business the right to produce its product together with its name, logos / brands in exchange for an initial fee and annual royalty payment (usually a percentage of the sales turnover or profit).

Foreign independent presence: involves a business actually setting up facilities in the chosen foreign market and operating from there.

Joint venture: where two businesses combine resources. In the case of international marketing it often involves the exporting firm joining with a locally based firm.

Standardisation (or globalisation): where a business entering a foreign market sells the same product / service abroad as sold in the domestic market and in the same way, ie with the same marketing strategy ie promotion, price, channel of distribution, etc

Adaptation (or localisation): where a business entering a foreign market adapts the marketing mix to suit local needs.

Potential Benefits:

- Survival from recession or saturation.
- The spreading of risk.
- Economies of scale.
- Enhanced image / status.
- Achievement of objectives re: sales, market share and / or profit & ROCE.

Potential Problems Challenges & Risks:

- Lack of knowledge, experience.
- Social, cultural, religious, language differences.
- Political differences.
- Legal differences.
- Differences in business practices and customs.
- Economic factors.
- Absence of, and the need to build trust with, locally based firms.
- Lack of customer awareness.
- Additional and increased costs.
- Problems with coordination and control.

Ways of Minimising the Risks:

- In-depth research and analysis.
- Appointing staff experienced in the market.
- Drawing up a detailed business plan.
- Minimising investment in fixed assets.
- Setting up any new firm as a limited Co.
- Taking out adequate insurance.
- Adequate training and supervision of staff.
- A stepped / incremental approach.

© **APT Initiatives Ltd**, 2009

Methods of Entry:

Keep production in home country and export:

- **Direct exporting** – foreign intermediary distributes product.
- **Indirect exporting** – sell goods to export company which undertakes research and identification of distribution channels: lower costs and risk. *But…* lower revenues.

Production in foreign market:

- **Licensing** – foreign firm obtains licence to sell product for a fee.
- **Franchising** – individual / firm buys right to produce product and use the name, logo and brand: fast access to foreign market without significant investment.
- **Foreign independent presence** – set up facilities abroad: cheaper labour, GVT incentives, lower transport costs, no import / exchange barriers, greater revenues as no 3rd party. *However…* **riskier** – greater **investment.**
- **Joint venture** – 2 companies combine resources: risk shared, draw upon each other's strengths. *But…* scope for conflict.

Factors to Consider when Deciding Method of Entry:

Internal:

- Corporate objectives and strategy.
- Nature of the product.
- Costs, profitability; Financial resources.
- HR – experience, expertise.
- Attitude to, and ability to cope with, risk.
- Willingness to share control.

External:

- Size and spread of the market.
- Needs / expectations of customers.
- Social and economic conditions.
- Competition.
- Political and legal factors.
- Availability and reputation of distributors.

Standardisation or Adaptation?

Key strategic decision: sell the same product / service abroad as sold in domestic market in same way ie same marketing strategy? (**standardisation** or **globalisation**), or adapt the marketing mix to suit local needs? (**adaptation** or **localisation**).

Potential Advantages / Disadvantages:

- **Standardisation:** less expensive - can benefit from economies in product development, purchasing, marketing. *But…*
- **Adaptation:** may be essential to meet the needs and tastes of customers in the chosen market in order to maximise sales.

The business must weigh up the cost of adapting the marketing mix (including loss in economies) against the potential benefits in terms of increased sales.

Conclusion:

Depends on:

- The nature of the product.
- Customer expectations.
- Objectives.
- The resources available.

Where customer needs, market conditions are fundamentally the same: **standardised** (globalised) approach.

Where market conditions, tastes, needs are radically different: **adaptation** (localisation).

Assessing Effectiveness of Marketing Strategies

Assessing effectiveness of marketing strategies: involves measuring the extent to which a particular strategy has achieved the objective it was implemented to achieve.

Criteria for Evaluation Strategy:

Strategy should be evaluated in terms of:

1. **Suitability** – for achieving objectives or addressing problems / weaknesses.
2. **Acceptability** – to key stakeholders.
3. **Feasibility** – of implementation, eg does the business have the resources?

Assessing the effectiveness of marketing strategies requires judgement over the extent to which the strategy achieved what it set out to achieve.

The Need for SMART Objectives:

A marketing strategy is a plan / course of action decided upon to achieve marketing objectives.

Thus, to measure the effectiveness of marketing strategy, objectives should be specific, measurable and timescaled ie **quantifiable.**

Once quantifiable targets have been set, properly designed monitoring and control systems should highlight where:

- objectives / targets are not being achieved.
- investigation is required.
- corrective action is required.

The Need for Market Research:

Evaluation of results may involve:

- direct feedback from customers.
- observation of competitor responses.

This research should regularly be reviewed together with sales and financial data and **corrective action** taken as required.

It requires understanding and reacting to internal and external factors. This might involve a minor change to one aspect of the marketing mix, or a complete change in strategy.

External Factors:

Firms are affected by internal and external, uncontrollable factors that can render targets out of date or difficult to achieve.

A firm must take these into account when measuring the effectiveness of strategy and forming judgements about performance.

© **APT Initiatives Ltd**, 2009

DEVELOPING AND IMPLEMENTING MARKETING PLANS

Components of Marketing Plans

Marketing Plan: a report outlining a firm's marketing objectives, strategies and tactics, including costings, timings and forecast results. It is part of a business's overall corporate plan and should take into account the business's corporate objectives, its internal capabilities, and external opportunities and threats.

Marketing strategy: a broad plan of action for achieving marketing objectives.

Marketing tactics: short term measures used to implement strategy.

Objectives – *Eg:* brand awareness, sales, market share, repeat business. Should be based on corporate objectives and be SMART.

Sales Forecasts (in terms of volume or value) help plan the use of resources eg material purchases, labour, production scheduling, distribution, cash flow. This is vital to ensure customer needs, expectations are met and objectives laid down in the plan are achieved.

Marketing Planning Process:

Gather info on present situation
– *Where are we now?*

↓

Evaluate present situation
– Conduct a SWOT Analysis

↓

Make predictive Assumptions

↓

Set Marketing Objectives
– *Where do we want to be?*

↓

Devise the Strategy & Tactics
– *How are we going to get there?*

↓

Implement the Strategy
(using Marketing Mix)

↓

Monitor / Review / Measure the Results – *Are we succeeding?*

Marketing strategy and tactics – expressed in marketing mix:

- Product / Service – key features, quality, branding, packaging.
- Price – to make a profit, which customers are willing to pay.
- Place – location; how product accessed / distribution channels.
- Promotion – to raise awareness, encourage purchase.

Some firms focus on one aspect, but **all** aspects remain important and need addressing. Customers need a product / service that:

- meets their needs (product).
- they can afford / provides value (price).
- they are fully aware of (promotion).
- they can access conveniently (place).

Need to blend mix to achieve desired result – sales, share, profit.

Costings / Budgets: an important means of control. Marketing budgets include targets for income and expenditure eg on: R&D, market research, warehousing & distribution, promotion, sales force, training & development of marketing staff, equipment. Budgets are generally produced annually but for control purposes are broken down into monthly targets for income and expenditure.

Implementation Schedule / Timings:

Who is responsible for doing *what* by *when?* Important for control – enables progress to be monitored and corrective action to be taken.

Contingency Plans:

The best plans also identify possible problems and action to overcome these - to help ensure the business achieves its objectives.

Assessing Internal and External Influences on Marketing Plans

Internal influences: factors that stem from inside the business that affect decisions over, or success in achieving, marketing plans.

External influences: factors that stem from outside the business that affect decisions over or success in achieving, marketing plans.

Internal Influences:

- Corporate objectives.
- Finance available.
- Skills and ability of the workforce.
- Capabilities of plant, equipment.

External Influences:

- Customer needs, wants.
- Competitors' actions, S & W.
- Legislation.
- Social attitudes.
- Economic.
- Technological.

Taking into account internal and external factors is essential to ensure:

- realistic marketing objectives and strategy.
- fair and appropriate judgements / modifications are made at the review stage.

Issues in Implementing Marketing Plans

Issues in Implementing Plans:

- The need for in-depth research and analysis and the resources and costs involved.
- Lack of research or consideration of external factors - can lead to variance in sales forecasts / budgets and devalue the plan.
- Lack of research or consideration of internal factors - can lead to insufficient resources to implement the plan.
- Failure to liaise with other functions - may result in insufficient cash or people of the right type, quality to carry out the plan.
- Failure to involve key staff at planning - can lead to lack of understanding of the requirements of the plan, problems at the implementation stage, including a lack of commitment.
- Changes in the internal or external environment - may affect implementation or appropriateness in achieving objectives.
- Treating plan as rigid document - can stifle initiative, result in slow reaction to change and missed business opportunities.

Concluding Comments – Marketing Plans:

Help maximise the performance and potential of a business.

The marketing planning process ensures strategies are properly thought through, researched. The completed plan:

- helps prioritise and allocate resources / responsibilities to meet customer requirements and fulfil marketing objectives.
- provides targets that can be used to monitor performance and enable timely action to be taken as necessary.
- can aid motivation (if communicated to staff) by providing a sense of direction, purpose and urgency.

The construction of a plan does not guarantee success – external factors outside a business's control can impinge upon its performance. Plans should, therefore, change as circumstances change to allow the business to react to and stave off threats, and take up opportunities.

© **APT Initiatives Ltd**, 2009

OPERATIONAL STRATEGIES

UNDERSTANDING OPERATIONAL OBJECTIVES

Operational Objectives

Operational objectives: goals or targets that must be achieved by the operations function within a business in order to achieve the business's corporate objectives. They provide a focus for decision making and for setting and agreeing operational strategies and plans.

SMART Operational Objectives:

To aid motivation, enable performance to be measured and provide an important means of control, like all objectives, operational objectives should be SMART and state by how much something should be reduced / increased, by what date.

Quality

Meeting customer needs, consistently – Requires:

- a market orientation.
- good quality supplies.
- capable processes.
- effective, committed people.

Eg Quality targets may concern:

- reducing rejects.
- improving reliability – delivery.
- reducing complaints.
- customer satisfaction.

Important to:

- secure repeat business.
- generate new customers.
- keep / improve competitiveness.
- minimise costs.
- maximise sales, profits.

Costs

Will involve targets relating to:

- materials, energy, labour, maintenance.
- direct costs, fixed costs, unit costs.

The bulk of costs stem from operations, thus, poor cost control has a major effect on profit.

It is central to the achievement of corporate objectives re: profit, return on investment.

Sourcing Products

Targets are increasingly common due to:

- the move towards service industries.
- ethical issues.

Eg: Increase % of products sourced from fair trade countries by x% by x date.

Volume & Capacity Utilisation

Stem from corporate and marketing objectives re: customer base, sales, share.

Targets may concern:

- producing X items in X amount of time.
- serving X customers in X amount of time.
- achieving growth in either of the above.

Capacity utilisation:

$$\frac{\text{Output per period}}{\text{Maximum possible output}} \times 100$$

Maximising capacity is important to keep fixed costs per unit down.

Increasing volumes may also provide economies of scale (considered later).

Innovation – *the successful implementation of new ideas* - eg targets re:

- spending on R & D.
- developing new products / processes.
- securing patents.
- launching products, brands.

© **APT Initiatives Ltd**, 2009

Efficiency – *Minimising wastage of resources, including time.*

Measured in terms of unit (average) costs, or time taken to undertake a process. The efficiency of a specific input or process can also be measured – *for example:*

- Labour – quantity per employee.
- Capital equipment – quantity per machine.
- Production process – percentage waste.

Targets may concern:

- producing X number of products or serving X customers in a given time.
- increasing products produced or customers served by X per cent.
- reducing the average time taken to produce a product or serve a customer.
- reducing the percentage of waste materials generated in the process.

May involve investment in:

- new technology, training, incentives (labour).
- preventative maintenance (machinery).

Can lead to lower average costs and, thus, increase the business's:

- profits / return.
- pricing flexibility / competitiveness - resulting in greater sales, market share.
- chance of survival in longer-term.

Environment:

Minimising the negative effect on the environment eg air, land, water pollution.

Targets may concern recycling and reducing:

- carbon emissions.
- water pollutants.
- energy use.
- other waste products.

May involve investment in:

- more modern energy efficient machinery.
- better stock control to reduce waste.
- raising staff awareness, training.
- alternative materials for packaging.

Cost may be balanced by:

- better image – greater sales, capital, easier recruitment.
- more efficient production – competitive.

Assessing Internal and External Influences on Operational Objectives

Internal influences: factors stemming from inside the business that can affect decisions over, or success in achieving, operational objectives.

External influences: factors stemming from outside the business that can affect decisions over, or success in achieving, operational objectives.

Internal Influences:

- The nature of the product.
- Corporate objectives.
- Other functional objectives.
- The finance available.
- Productive capacity and capability.
- Strength of worker representation.

External Influences:

- Consumer needs and expectations.
- Market and demand factors.
- Competitor activities.
- Economic factors.
- Political and legal factors.
- Social influences.
- Technological change.
- Suppliers – cost, quality, reliability, flexibility.

SCALE AND RESOURCE MIX

Choosing the Right Scale of Production: Economies & Diseconomies of Scale

Scale of production: concerns a business's level of output which depends upon its capacity.
Capacity: the maximum level of output a business can produce within a given period of time using its present resources.
Economies of scale: factors that lead to a reduction in unit costs as a business increases its output / size and scale of operations.
Diseconomies of scale: factors that cause unit costs to rise as a business increases its output / size and scale of operations.
Unit cost / average cost: the total cost (ie fixed and variable) divided by the number of units produced.
External economies and diseconomies of scale: arise when an entire industry grows in size.

Choosing the Right Scale:

A key decision which largely depends on the nature and level of demand.

If capacity is too **high** in relation to demand this:

- wastes resources - idle machinery, staff.
- increases fixed costs per unit.
- reduces profitability.

If capacity is too **low** in relation to demand this can result in:

- long waits for orders - dissatisfied customers, financial penalties.
- less time for routine maintenance - breakdowns, delays.
- cramped conditions, fewer breaks - mistakes, returns, absence, accidents.
- falling morale, motivation - increased absence, labour turnover.

If a business has a capacity shortage and demand is growing in the long-term, the decision to increase scale will depend upon the business's ability to secure the resources eg finance, labour, etc required.

As scale increases: up to a certain point the firm may benefit from **economies** of scale, after which the firm may suffer from **diseconomies**.

Economies of Scale:

As a business increases its output unit costs reduce mainly because fixed costs (which stay the same in the short-run) are spread over a greater number of units. Unit costs may also be lower due to other economies of scale eg:

- **Purchasing** - bulk purchase discounts.
- **Technical** - afford more modern machinery - quicker, more reliable; flow production - unskilled, no delays.
- **Specialisation** - staff become expert, need less training.

Diseconomies of Scale:

Beyond a certain point a firm may encounter problems with:

- **Communication** – more levels, slower decisions.
- **Coordination and control** - more difficult - requires regular meetings, checking procedures - increase costs.

More likely when expansion is rapid and systems are not developed in time to cope with the pressures of growth.

© **APT Initiatives Ltd**, 2009

Choosing the Optimal Mix of Resources: Capital & Labour Intensity

Capital or labour intensity: the degree to which the production of a product or service relies more upon the use of capital or labour.

Capital intensive production: uses a high proportion of capital resources (plant, machinery, vehicles, equipment, IT) relative to labour. It is common to large scale production and flow production systems.

Labour intensive production: uses a high proportion of labour relative to capital resources. Thus, labour costs are a high proportion of total costs. It is common to individual, personalised products / services, small scale production and job or batch production systems.

Job production: where a single item is made or order is processed, from start to finish, usually according to the customer's specifications. It usually involves 'one-off', unique orders which may or may not be repeated.

Batch production: where a large or small quantity (batch) of the same item is produced at the same time. It does not involve the continuous production of items (as with flow production).

Flow production: the continuous production of a large quantity of items.

Mass production: where large volumes of identical products are made to the same standard.

Capital Intensive Strategies:

Benefits – Machines - quicker, more reliable:

- minimise lead times.
- minimise costs from poor quality.
- allow more ambitious targets re: quality, volume, efficiency.

They may also produce technically superior products - increasing competitiveness, sales.

Drawbacks – Costs:

- Set up costs: purchase, installation, training.
- Ongoing costs: maintenance, depreciation.

However, costs can be minimised through renting / leasing. *Plus,* the longer-term benefits ie quality, efficiency should outweigh the costs.

Labour Intensive:

Benefits:

- No up-front capital outlay.
- Lower fixed costs.
- More flexible than machines.
- Social – job creation.

Drawbacks:

- More complex to manage.
- Ongoing effort and investment to attract, motivate and retain staff.
- More vulnerable to external factors.

Moving from labour to capital intensive:

- Temporary disruption, delays.
- Redundancies – pay, morale.
- De-skilling – job satisfaction.
- Problem learning to use machinery – anxiety.
- Workforce resistance (due to the above).
- Negative publicity – affect sales in short-term.

Requires: careful planning and MGT of change.

Factors Influencing Choice:

- Nature of the product.
- Customer expectations.
- Level of demand.
- Availability of capital and labour.
- Relative cost.
- Age, size, financial position of the business.

INNOVATION

Innovation, Research and Development

Innovation: the successful implementation of a new idea eg new product, process, approach, strategy. It should be distinguished from creativity and invention. Creativity concerns idea generation. Invention is a technical process of perfecting an idea. Innovation requires ideas to be put into action and is concerned with the commercial application of the idea or invention.

Research and development: Research is the study of a particular subject or market in order to further knowledge in this subject or market; development is the application of this knowledge resulting in new products or ways of doing things.

Value analysis: a process which seeks to cut the costs of producing a product without reducing the 'value' from the customer's perspective, and / or increasing the value of a particular product (in the eyes of the customer) without increasing the production costs.

Innovation:

*The successful implementation of **new** ideas, eg the…*

- launch of a new product.
- application of a new process.
- implementation of a new strategy.

It does **not** just concern NPD or something **totally** new.

Whatever the type / level of innovation, it should lead to **increased value** for the customer and / or the business.

Innovation differs from **creativity** (idea generation) and **invention** (the technical process for perfecting an idea). It is the **commercial application** of the idea / invention.

It is driven by:

- changes in demand (demand pull).
- technological (push) breakthroughs.

Research & Development:

A key activity associated with innovation.

R&D activities:

- Researching new ideas.
- Inventing, designing, testing, developing new ideas.
- Developing prototypes.
- Modifying existing products, processes.
- Gaining feedback.

The Stages Involved

Identification of new ideas

↓

Screening and selection of new ideas

↓

Detailed investigation of new ideas

↓

Pilot production / Prototype

↓

Testing and Review

↓

Full Launch

© **APT Initiatives Ltd**, 2009

Implications for Other Functions:

Finance: *Innovation…*

- can be expensive, time consuming.
- needs to budgeted for.
- may involve lengthy payback period.
- may require investment appraisal prior to funding full launch.

Marketing: *Innovation…*

- requires market research on customers, competitors.
- is often linked to product life cycles.

Thus, close liaison between marketing and R&D required to ensure timely development and implementation of extension strategies and new / replacement products.

HR: *Innovation…*

- might involve changes to working practices and / or retraining.
- can be unsettling for the workforce.
- needs careful, sensitive handling.

Purpose, Costs, Benefits and Risks of Innovation

Purpose and Benefits:

- **Improve quality or increase value** – improved quality may help improve a business's reputation, attract customers, maximise sales and gain market share, and / or enable a higher price to be charged, thereby maximising profitability.
- **Extend the life of a product** – to maintain sales and / or market share.
- **Extend the product range** – to expand the customer base and increase sales and / or ensure a balanced product portfolio.
- **Replace declining products** – to maintain sales and profits.
- **Respond to competitors** – to maintain sales, market share.
- **Enter or create a new market** – making a firm less vulnerable to changes in its existing market(s) or allowing it to more easily achieve growth or profit objectives.
- **Use spare capacity, increase utilisation** – keeping down fixed costs per unit.
- **Reduce costs, increase efficiency** eg through new materials or processes – providing the business with greater flexibility over price and / or higher margins.
- **Reduce impact on environment** eg through new packaging or processes – to create a positive image / publicity, attract customers, employees and investors.
- **Comply with legislation** – to avoid financial penalties, negative publicity.

Costs and Risks:

- Cost of R&D.
- Cost of launch / implementation.
- High failure rate.
- High cost of failure (not just financial).
- External factors – success not guaranteed.
- Ease with which ideas can be copied.
- Impact on the workforce.

Despite the costs & risks innovation is essential in the modern business world. Continual investment is increasingly important due to:

- increased competition.
- rapidly changing technology.
- higher customer expectations.

LOCATION

Methods of Making Location Decisions

Quantitative factors: factors that can be measured in some way.

Qualitative factors: factors that concern people's attitudes, beliefs, feelings, opinions, perceptions, values and prior experience.

Investment appraisal - in the context of location decisions: involves comparisons between cash inflows (revenues) and cash outflows (costs) at different locations. It concerns the speed at which the actual investment involved in locating at a particular site is paid back, or the rate of return on the investment.

Break-even analysis - in the context of location decisions: involves examining the behaviour of costs and revenues in relation to the output likely to be achieved at different locations, and predicting what is likely to happen with regard to profit at these different locations.

Qualitative Factors

- Image.
- Tradition.
- Labour relations.
- Owner's preference.
- Quality of life.

Quantitative Factors:

- Availability & cost of land, premises.
- Availability & cost of capital.
- Availability & cost of labour.
- Access / proximity to supplies.
- Government incentives.
- Access / proximity to customers.
- Infrastucture.
- Location of competitors.
- State of the local economy.
- Relocation costs (adjacent).

Relocation costs: *May include:*

- Notifying stakeholders.
- Changing business stationery.
- Redundancies.
- Lost production during move.
- Interest on loan to fund re-location.

The **nature of the business** will determine the importance of each factor, eg:

- Traditional retail business – needs to be located near to target customer base.
- Manufacturing firm – prime consideration will be minimising production costs.

Profit is the prime motive of **commercial** businesses and so the effect on fixed costs, variable costs and revenues will be paramount. *Thus…*

- higher costs may be justified if accompanied by proportionately higher revenues.
- lower revenues justified if accompanied by proportionately lower costs.

Non-profit making organisations eg public service still need to assess effect on fixed and variable costs, but revenue needs to be substituted with level of service. *Thus…*

- higher costs may be justified if accompanied with proportionately higher level of service.

© **APT Initiatives Ltd**, 2009

Quantitative Techniques of Analysis:

Break-even: If a business is able to break-even faster at one location than another = lower risk. But this might not mean more profit – depends on cost structure ie the weighting between fixed costs (FC) and variable costs (VC). *Example:*

Cost / Rev / Profit	Site X	Site Y
FC per annum	£600,000	£860,000
VC per unit	£8	£6
Selling price per unit	£14	£14
Breakeven (units) (FC/Contribution)	**100,000**	**107,500**
Expected Demand	190,000	180,000
Forecast Profit	**£540,000** (90k x £6)	**£580,000** (72.5k x £8)

X: lower b-even, larger market. **Y:** greater profit.

Also consider when Site Y becomes more profitable…

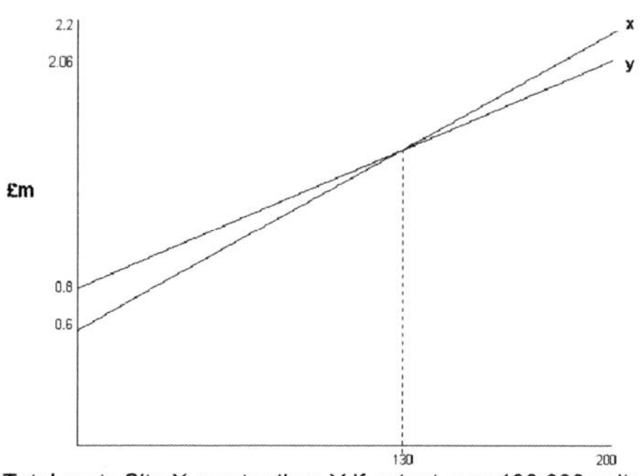

Total costs Site X greater than Y if output over 130,000 units. Once 130,000 reached, business more profitable at Site Y. Must assess likelihood of meeting 130,000 plus consistently.

Investment Appraisal:

If a site has not been purchased - there is no initial outlay, ARR and payback is irrelevant. But discounted cash flow (NPV) can be used to appraise the location.

If a business **relocates** it will have moving and communication costs (notifying stakeholders), and, possibly, redundancy payments. Thus, it will be possible to use all 3 investment appraisal techniques.

Benefits of the Optimal Location

The optimal location: The location where the benefits (financial or otherwise) outweigh the costs (financial or otherwise).

Benefits of the Optimal Location:

- Lower costs – fixed and / or variable costs.
- Greater revenue or level of service eg improved access to customers or resources – enabling faster response to customer needs.
- Greater profits, thus, greater ROCE, return to shareholders and / or funds for re-investment.

The optimal location will ultimately be the one that helps the business to achieve its **prime** objective. *Thus for…*

- **Private profit making** – the optimal location will be the one that maximises **profit.**
- **Non-profit making, public sector** – the optimal location will minimise **costs** and / or maximise the **service** provided.

The Advantages and Disadvantages of Multi-site Locations

Site: a physical location of a business. **Single site:** one physical location. **Multi-site:** the occupation by a business of more than one physical location. This may involve sites in the same or different grounds, town, city, county or country.

Multi-nationals: businesses operating sites in more than one country.

Advantages: A multi-site location may:

- permit specialisation.
- spread risk.
- enable growth.
- improve service to customers.
- secure lower costs.
- avoid some diseconomies of scale.
- minimise disruption of existing operations.
- be cheaper than expansion on existing site
- provide greater flexibility.

Disadvantages: Some advantages can also be disadvantages, eg specialisation by plant could lead to:

- duplication of resources / facilities.
- increased stockholding costs.

The most common disadvantages:

- more difficult to manage - problems with communication, coordination, control.
- potential loss in economies of scale.

Minimising the Problems:

Eg by establishing:

- a clear mission, aims, objectives - communicated throughout all levels.
- a clear structure - with clear lines of accountability, responsibility and reporting procedures.
- regular communication - to clarify requirements, expectations, outcomes.

Issues Relating to International Location

Off-shoring: the relocation of a business process eg manufacturing, customer service, accounting, from one country to another.

Protectionism: a policy of protecting domestic producers by imposing barriers such as quotas and tariffs on imports.

Quotas: limits on the amount that can be imported in a country.

Tariffs: fees levied on goods imported into a country.

Reasons for International Location:

To:

- sell to overseas markets – achieve growth, survive recession, or saturation in domestic markets.
- secure lower costs.
- **both** of the above.

Issues with International Location:

- Currency fluctuations.
- Barriers to trade eg quotas, tariffs.
- Transport costs.
- Utility costs.
- Legal differences.
- Differences in tax.
- Political stability.
- Social, cultural, religious, language differences.
- Ethical issues.
- Managerial control – more difficult.

© APT Initiatives Ltd, 2009

LEAN PRODUCTION

Introduction to Lean Production

Waste: *Stems from…*

- using more resources than necessary.
- mistakes.
- overproducing.
- carrying excessive stocks.
- using more space than required.
- spending more than necessary.
- using more people than necessary.
- excess time on product development.
- unnecessary movement, transport.

Lean production: minimising the use of key business resources (ie materials, labour, capital, factory floor space, time) and eliminating waste without reducing customer value.

Waste: any activity that adds to costs but not to value.

Lean Production Tools / Techniques:

- cell production.
- just in time production.
- kaizen groups.
- simultaneous engineering.
- critical path analysis.

Benefits:

Minimise costs as: uses less time, labour, stock, factory space, capital equipment.

Maximise quality as: result in fewer defects and quicker production / delivery / service.

Requirements:

- close relations with suppliers.
- multi-skilled workforce.
- Committed, motivated staff.
- willingness to accept change.
- trust, co-operation not conflict
- management by consent.

The Effective Management of Time

Time-based management: involves using time periods and time deadlines as a basis for decision-making. Instead of focusing on the output the business deliberately targets time issues eg lead time between idea conception to product development and launch, lead time between an order being received and delivered to the customer, lead time for a business to receive an order from a supplier.

Lead time: the length of time taken between two or more processes.

Simultaneous engineering: involves organising the processes / stages involved in product development in such a way as to enable the different stages to be carried out simultaneously ie at the same time, as opposed to one after the other.

CAD (Computer Aided Design): allows a business to simulate the product on a computer screen and alter the specification, colour, features, in order to change the design, without ever having to build a prototype, thus minimising design costs.

CAM (Computer Aided Manufacture): uses computers to control and adjust the production process. It allows firms to manufacture products in shorter times, with improved quality and reliability, and thus, lower costs.

Benefits:

Time-based MGT can:

- increase productivity.
- reduce costs.
- enhance customer satisfaction.
- increase competitiveness.
- maximise sales & market share.
- maximise profitability.
- improve cash flow.

Achieving Shorter Product Development Times

May involve **simultaneous engineering** and the use of multi-disciplined teams and can:

- generate more ideas.
- enable faster feedback / response.
- provide clear understanding of constraints
- ensure products designed 'right first time'.

Computer-Aided Design (**CAD**): can view 3-d image of prototype, without lengthy, expensive process of building models.

Shorter Production Lead Times

Computer-**A**ided **M**anufacture – computers control and adjust the production process – manufacture products in shorter times, with improved quality, reliability, lower costs.

Where **consumers' tastes change rapidly** and there is **strong competition**, emphasis on shorter product development and production lead times may be essential to maintain / increase competitiveness, maximise sales and market share.

Assessing the Value of Critical Path Analysis

Critical path analysis: involves displaying all the activities involved in a particular project in diagrammatical form, so as to communicate exactly when the resources are required and for how long. It allows a business to estimate the shortest possible time in which a project can be completed and identifies those activities that must be completed on time in order to avoid delaying the entire project (ie the activities that form part of the critical path). It is used for complex projects such as building and construction, as well as marketing plans involving research, advertising and test marketing.

Critical activities: activities that must be completed on time in order to avoid delaying an entire project.

Non-critical activities: activities that can be delayed up to a certain point without delaying the completion of an entire project.

Drawing Simple Networks:

Nodes: Represent the start and finish of an activity. All network diagrams start and finish on a single node.

Arrows: Represent an activity that has a duration. Run from left to right. The length has no bearing on the activity's duration.

Steps to Produce a Network Diagram:

1. Identify **activities** that make up the project.
2. Determine for each activity **what activities:**
   a) need completing before they can start.
   b) depend on completion of the activity.
   c) the duration of the activity.

© **APT Initiatives Ltd**, 2009

Example:

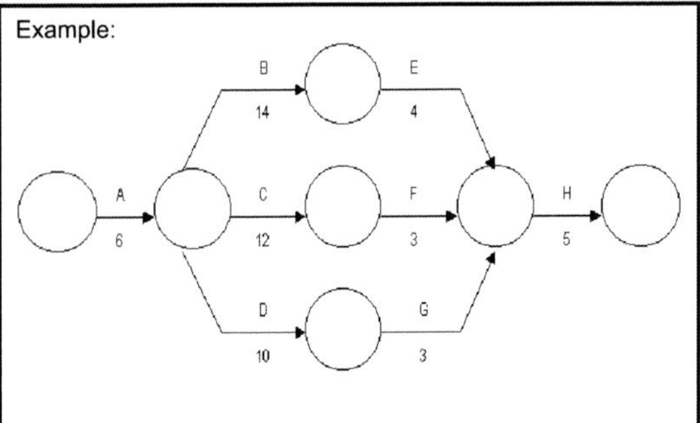

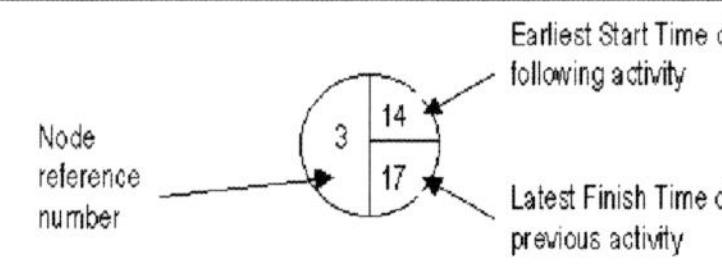

Node ref. No - allocated in logical manner - usually from left to right.

Earliest Start Time of each activity: the earliest time an activity may begin - depends on duration of previous dependent activities.

Minimum duration of the project: the earliest time the project may finish, given the sequence and duration of all the activities.

Latest Finish Time of each activity: latest time activity must finish to ensure the entire project finishes within the minimum duration time.

Determining EST's & Minimum Length of Project:

1. Place 0 in the upper right hand segment of node 1.
2. Add duration of each activity to EST of this activity to give EST of next.

NB If more than 1 activity is entering a node, the **highest** EST figure must be taken (see diagram adjacent and Node 6).

Minimum length of project = EST in the final node.

Determining LFT's:

1. Give last node of the project an LFT equal to its EST.
2. Working backwards from right to left, subtract the length of the activity from the LFT of the node at the point of the arrow, to get the LFT at the node of the start of the arrow.

NB Where a node has more than 1 arrow starting from it, the **lowest** figure is chosen (see diagram adjacent and Node 2).

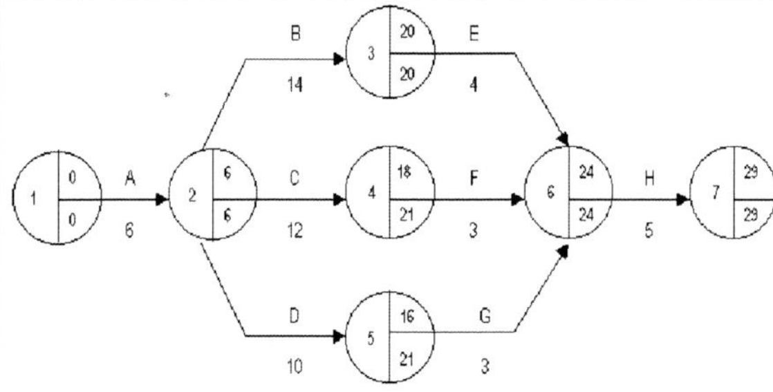

EST's Node 6: Activity G ends by 19 (16+3 - see Node 5), activity F by 21, E by 24, thus 24 inserted – as H cannot start until all 3 activities are completed. Hence minimum duration of this project is 29 days.

LFT's Node 2: Although in Node 5 LFT of D is 21, and 21 – 10 = 11, if 11 was inserted into Node 2 LFT, the project would be delayed: counting from B to E to H would take it to 34 (11+14+4+5).

Calculating Total Float: how long an activity can be extended or postponed so that the project still finishes within the minimum duration time. Calculated by:

LFT – Duration – EST (of an individual activity)

Activity	LFT	Duration	EST	Total Float
A	6	6	0	0
B	20	14	6	0
C	21	12	6	3
D	21	10	6	5
E	24	4	20	0
F	24	3	18	3
G	24	3	16	5
H	29	5	24	0

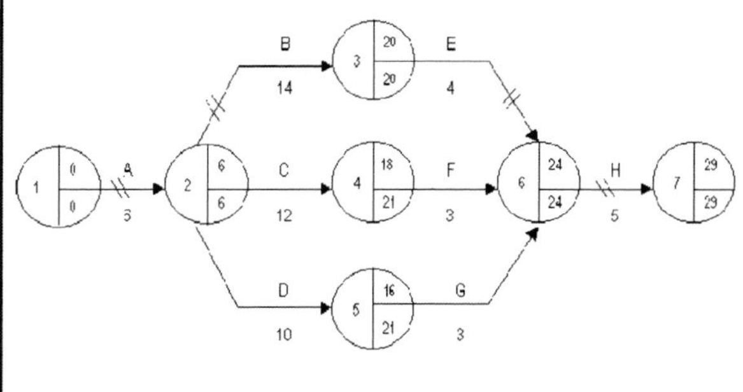

Identifying the Critical Path:

Activities with a total float of 0 cannot be delayed without delaying the entire project. They represent the critical path – A, B, E, H.
On the diagram they are where the EST's equal EFT's. Two parallel lines are drawn through these activities to represent the critical path.

Role, Purpose, Benefits of CPA:

- Estimating and minimising project completion time.
- Costing and selecting projects.
- Planning and organising resources.
- Prioritising resources.
- Motivating staff.
- Monitoring and controlling activities.

Criticisms of CPA:

- Relies on estimates.
- Requires significant planning and time.
- Can lead to tight deadlines – encourage staff to cut corners, *resulting in…*
- Timely completion at expense of quality.

Overall, however, CPA can help to:

- minimise wastage of resources.
- maximise profitability.
- ensure customer satisfaction.
- provide a competitive edge.

© **APT Initiatives Ltd**, 2009

Effective Management of Other Resources through Methods of Lean Production

Just-in-time (JIT) production: a philosophy of producing products, whereby materials and components arrive at the workplace in such a way that the time lag between their arrival and work taking place is minimised and very little, if any, (buffer) stock is kept in case of problems with delivery or work in progress, etc. It also applies to the finished product, because once the product has been made it is despatched immediately to the customer.

Cell production: involves dividing the production process amongst small teams or 'cells'. Workers within each cell may operate on one or a group of functions of the production process, and are given responsibility for every part of the product and production process during the time that the work-in-progress passes through the cell. Responsibility may include task allocation, quality control, health and safety, purchasing of supplies, and stock control.

Kaizen: a Japanese word that means continuous improvement. It usually involves groups of workers that meet regularly to discuss how work-related tasks can be completed more efficiently. Because workers are involved in the detailed operation of the business, they are considered to be sufficiently well qualified to be able to identify any problematic areas and suggest improvements.

Just-in-Time Production:

Potential Benefits:

Minimises stock levels and associated costs: storage, finance, opportunity cost, deterioration / obsolescence.

Also – as no surplus stock – helps to:

- maximise quality, minimise waste – due to the pressure to get perfect quality first time.
- highlights inefficiencies – resulting in improvements.

Other benefits:

- improves cash flow.
- frees up storage space for more productive use.
- increased staff motivation - from greater responsibility.

Potential Problems / Drawbacks:

- Vulnerable to changes in supply, machine breakdowns.
- Risk of orders not being met on time.
- Restricts ability to meet sudden increase in demand.

Requires:

- careful planning - sales forecasting.
- flexible, reliable suppliers.
- reliable machinery.
- able, motivated, committed staff - training, working conditions, pay, etc.

Other potential drawbacks:

- loss of bulk buying discounts.
- greater administration, ordering, handling.

Thus, the business should research whether the lower stock costs and reduction in waste compensates for any loss in discounts and outweigh the extra labour costs involved with handling a greater number of smaller deliveries.

Cell Production:

Potential Benefits:

- Reduced supervision – lower costs.
- Less waste, mistakes – lower costs.
- Enhanced motivation, lower labour turnover and associated costs due to…
- …increased job variety, responsibility (Herzberg's 'motivators').
- …small teams – social needs (Mayo).

Other advantages of team working:

- Better decisions – draw upon knowledge, skills of others.
- More willing to be innovative – as responsibility shared.
- Less disruption – members generally have the ability to perform each other's jobs.

Potential Drawbacks:

- Training – in a wider range of skills – costs.
- Possible requests for a pay increase.

Kaizen:

Benefits:

- Access to innovative ideas that reduce costs, improve quality.
- Enhanced motivation, productivity – staff feel valued, more fulfilled (esteem, self-actualisation needs).
- More positive relationships between management and staff (social needs).
- Easier implementation of decisions over improvements – as staff had some input in these decisions.
- Better quality decisions – staff know more about their jobs, plus a variety of opinions helps to identify faulty assumptions, errors or omissions, and the timely correction of these.

Drawback:

- Requires well-qualified staff to organise and initiate the kaizen groups.

But…

- The process of general discussion leading towards improvement on a continual basis should help to increase the quality of all staff who take part.

Closing Comments – Lean Production Techniques:

Implementing lean production techniques incurs costs eg training. *However…*

- Costs are generally short-term and outweighed by the significant savings and efficiencies gained in the longer-term.

© **APT Initiatives Ltd**, 2009

HUMAN RESOURCES STRATEGIES

UNDERSTANDING HR OBJECTIVES

HR Objectives

HR Objectives: goals or targets that must be achieved by the human resources function to achieve the corporate objectives.

Matching Workforce Skills, Size and Location to Business Needs:

Ensuring the right number and quality of staff are in the right place at the right time. This is vital to:

- meet customer needs.
- minimise labour costs.

Can be challenging – especially if the strategy to deal with a surplus involves redundancies.

This is an ongoing concern / objective for a seasonal business.

Minimising Labour Costs:

Particularly relevant to labour intensive firms. Might concern targets re:

- punctuality.
- absence / attendance.
- labour turnover / staff retention.

Each can be costly – *eg:*

- Absence: overtime, agency staff, sick pay.
- Labour turnover: advertise, interview, induct, train new staff.
- MGT time getting cover, extending deadlines.

HR MGT and the setting and the achievement of HR objectives are **part of every manager's job, irrespective of the function** in which the managers operate.

If a separate HR department exists, then it is their job to largely act in a coordinating and advisory role for operational managers.

Making Full Use of the Workforce's Potential:

Involves:

- Investment in training, development.
- Opportunity for promotion.

Can help:

- maximise job satisfaction.
- enhance motivation, commitment of staff.
- increase staff retention.
- reduce labour turnover and associated costs.

Maintaining Good Employer / Employee Relations:

Sound business practice – *It can…*

- enhance motivation, commitment - reduce absence, labour turnover and associated costs.
- encourage employees to air grievances - enable early resolution - minimise industrial action and associated costs.
- encourage employees to put forward ideas / suggestions.
- result in staff being more willing to accept changes in the workplace.
- create a positive corporate image - attract good staff, customers - sales.

© **APT Initiatives Ltd**, 2009

Internal and External Influences on HR Objectives

Internal influences: factors stemming from inside the business that can affect decisions over, or success in achieving, HR objectives.

External influences: factors stemming from outside the business that can affect decisions over, or success in achieving, HR objectives.

Internal Influences:

- Corporate strategy.
- Corporate objectives.
- Corporate culture.
- Other functional objectives, strategy.
- Financial position.
- Worker representation.
- Nature of product and workforce.

External Influences:

- State of the market, level / nature of demand.
- Competitor activities.
- Competition for labour from other firms.
- Interest, exchange, inflation, unemployment rate
- Government policy and legislation.
- Social, demographic factors including education.
- Technological developments.
- Trade unions.

HR Strategies

HR strategies: plans or courses of action decided upon to achieve the business's human resource objectives.

Hard HR strategies: focus on the tight control of employees in the pursuit of organisational objectives. They involve a systematic, rational approach to HR management – where quantitative factors take precedence over qualitative factors. The job to be done is seen to be far more important than the person doing it.

Soft HR strategies: seek to fulfil the needs of the individual as well as fulfil organisational goals. They focus on nurturing and developing employees in order to maximise their potential. They take into account qualitative factors ie the feelings, needs and emotions of individual employees when making decisions, in order to gain the trust and long-term commitment of employees.

Hard HR Strategies:

- Employees are expendable – to be managed as effectively and efficiently as possible.
- A systematic, rational approach to MGT – quantitative over qualitative factors.
- Job, deadlines – far more important than person doing it / meeting them.
- Employees highly directed, rarely consulted, closely monitored, supervised.
- Link: Taylor's Scientific Mgt, McGregor's Theory X, autocratic leadership.

Strengths – *May…*

- be easier to maintain control – get the job done to a high standard.
- be easier to implement measures to match workforce size to business needs.
- minimise labour costs – as minimum investment in training and development.
- be essential in times of crisis and when tight deadlines need to be met.

Weaknesses – *May…*

- alienate employees – not committed to organisational goals.
- de-motivate employees – lack of responsibility, participation – feel under-valued, unfulfilled.
- result in high labour turnover and associated costs.

Soft HR Strategies:

- Employees are a highly valuable asset – a source of competitive advantage.
- Seek to fulfil the needs of the individual <u>and</u> the organisation.
- Job <u>and</u> person doing it - both important.
- Staff consulted, given autonomy rather than forced to follow pre-set guidelines.
- Meaningful, interesting, varied jobs.
- Opportunities for development, promotion.
- Redeployment rather than redundancy.
- Link: human relations theory, McGregors Theory Y, democratic leadership.

Strengths – *May result in…*

- high staff morale, job satisfaction, motivation, *thus…*
- …greater commitment, productivity, reduced absence, lower labour turnover.
- …reputation as good employer – attract good quality employees.
- more creative, multi-skilled, flexible workforce.
- better quality and easier implementation of decisions - from consultation, participation.

Weaknesses:

- Slower decision making - consultation, participation.
- Greater potential for conflict, loss of control - staff air views, greater autonomy.
- Too much emphasis on 'soft' approach - deadlines over-run, falling productivity.
- Ongoing training, development costs.
- Greater risk of staff being poached.
- More difficult to adapt workforce to meet changing needs.

Appropriateness of Each Approach:

Depends upon:

- The nature of the business and the task to be performed.
- The nature of the workforce.
- The business situation.

Examples:

- Complex task, highly skilled staff – less expendable, higher expectations – **soft**.
- Staff prefer direction; do not have the knowledge or interest in making a contribution – **hard**.
- Firm's survival threatened, fast decision required – **hard**.

The two approaches are **not** incompatible. In the majority of circumstances a **balance** is required. This may involve:

- Making staff aware of business goals and how their work contributes to these.
- Giving guidelines / parameters whilst allowing staff to have a say.
- Knowing each person's abilities and matching them to project needs.
- Making sure staff have the resources to get the job done.
- Monitoring staff but not <u>every</u> activity.
- Listening to concerns and *explaining why* where issues cannot be resolved.
- Rewards that meet individual <u>and</u> business needs / goals.

© **APT Initiatives Ltd**, 2009

DEVELOPING AND IMPLEMENTING WORKFORCE PLANS

Components of Workforce Plans

Workforce plan: a report detailing a business's labour requirements over a certain period of time, and the action required to ensure the right number and type of people are in the right place at the right time to enable a business to carry out its planned activities and fulfil its objectives.

Workforce planning: involves determining the number and type of employees required, where and by when, to enable an organisation to carry out its planned activities and fulfil its objectives.

Workforce Planning – Key Stages:

1. **Supply Analysis:** Analyse & forecast internal supply, assess external supply.
2. **Demand Analysis:** Identify no. & type of staff for objectives, plans, demand.
3. **Gap Analysis:** Compare supply with demand to identify surpluses, shortages.
4. **Solution Analysis:** Identify, consider, select strategies for surplus, shortage.
5. **Implementation of Solutions.**
6. **Evaluation – Monitoring & Review.**

The Workforce Size, Skills & Location Required to Match Business Needs: *This first section should detail:*

- number and type (skills, qualities, qualifications, experience) of staff required in each part of the business and when they are required.
- any surpluses or shortfalls.

Strategies – *for a shortfall:*

- Overtime.
- Measures to increase productivity.
- External recruitment - competitive packages.
- Long-term training programmes.
- Internal promotion.
- Transfers in.
- Outsourcing.
- Mechanisation / automation.

Strategies – *for a surplus:*

- Reducing overtime.
- Short-time working.
- Reducing work subcontracted out.
- Redeploying, retraining, transfers out.
- Downsizing, delayering – **redundancies** (see adjacent)

Options – *in the case of* ***redundancies:***

- Firing the casual labour first.
- Natural wastage.
- Voluntary redundancy / early retirement.
- Compulsory redundancy (last resort).

Costings / Budgets:

Targets for expenditure – eg on advertising for recruitment, training, development, promotions, redundancies.

An important means of control.

Timing / Implementation Schedule:

State *who* is responsible for doing *what* by *when*. Important control mechanism – monitor progress, take timely corrective as required.

Contingencies:

The best plans will also include contingency plans – identifying possible problems / challenges and action to overcome these.

Assessing Internal and External Influences on Workforce Plans

Internal influences on workforce plans: factors coming from inside the business that can affect decisions over, or success in implementing, workforce plans.

External influences on workforce plans: factors stemming from outside the business that can affect decisions over, or success in implementing, workforce plans.

Internal Influences:

- The nature of the product / service.
- Corporate objectives and strategy.
- Objectives and strategy of other functional areas.
- The finance available.
- Labour productivity, rates of absenteeism and labour turnover.
- The size and strength of worker representation.

External Influences:

- Customer demand, market and economic factors.
- Packages offered by other businesses.
- Technological developments.
- Demographic and social change including the level of education, training.
- Wage rates.
- Government policy and legislation.
- Trade unions.

Changes in external factors (and internal factors) can be difficult to predict. Hence, **flexibility** needs to be built into the plan to ensure:

- timely response to any changes affecting its implementation, and / or;
- the plan's appropriateness in meeting business needs.

© **APT Initiatives Ltd**, 2009

Issues in Implementing Workforce Plans

Employer / ee Relations:

Eg: short-time working, redundancies can negatively affect this.

Costs:

Eg: recruitment, selection, induction, training, re-deployment, redundancy.

Training / Retraining:

- of new recruits; H&S training required by law.
- in new products, processes, redeployment.

Treating the Plan as a Rigid Document:

- Factors outside control affect the plan's implementation / appropriateness.

Corporate Image:

- Layoffs, redundancies - negatively affect reputation as employer and customers' perceptions - may negatively affect sales.
- New jobs - enhance image - reverse effect.

- Predicting the behaviour of employees, customers and external events is not an easy task – requires constant monitoring.
- Figures on type, skills of employees must be checked, revised and regularly updated as factors change.
- Changes must be well thought out, especially redundancies as these can lead to industrial relations problems, affect the morale and motivation of staff and, ultimately, the business's performance.

The Value of Using Workforce Plans

Value:

The **planning process** is as important as the completed plan. *It…*

- ensures requirements thoroughly researched, strategies properly thought through.
- helps predict / anticipate shortfalls / surpluses – allows time to plan to ensure business needs are met.

The **completed plan**…

- provides comprehensive framework which guides operations and decision making.
- helps prioritise and allocate resources to meet customer and business needs.
- helps maximise productivity & profitability - eliminates surpluses which add to costs.
- provides targets to monitor performance - enables timely, appropriate action.

Limitations:

- Dependent upon accuracy of forecasts.
- Factors outside a firm's control affect its ability to secure the labour required.
- Even if the plan is based on in-depth analysis, unpredictable external factors can affect the plan's validity.

Although the construction of a plan does not guarantee success, failure to plan will greatly increase the chance of failure.

COMPETITIVE ORGANISATIONAL STRUCTURES

Types of Organisational Structure and Factors Determining Choice

Organisational structure: the way in which an organisation's activities are grouped together and coordinated to ensure members work together to achieve organisational goals.

Departmentalisation: dividing and grouping an organisation's activities into distinct tasks or sets of tasks.

Hierarchy: the order of levels of management or supervisors within a business, from the lowest to the highest.

Span of control: the number of people reporting directly to a particular manager or supervisor (or the number of people for whom a manager or supervisor is directly responsible).

Formalisation: the drawing up of written policies, rules, regulations, job descriptions and standing orders, etc which prescribe the correct or expected action of members of an organisation.

Functional organisational structure: where staff are grouped into different departments / functional areas which perform a common set of activities eg Marketing and Operations.

Divisional organisational structure: where staff are grouped around product / service lines, or customer groups, or geographical locations.

Matrix organisational structure: combines both functional and product or market structures. For example, staff are organised into project teams that consist of people involved in a particular function, as well as people involved in a particular product or customer group. Each employee reports to both a functional or divisional manager and to a project manager.

Mechanistic organisational structure: has a high degree of formalisation, many layers in the hierarchy, narrow spans of control and highly centralised decision making.

Organic organisational structure: has few rigid rules and regulations, few hierarchical levels, wide spans of control, and low centralisation, with people often allowed to use their own initiative.

Technology: the combination of skills, knowledge, tools, equipment, machines and computers used to carry out a business's planned activities.

Overview:

Coordinating the activities of members essentially occurs through:

- **informal communication** channels.
- the development of a **formal hierarchy** with clearly defined **spans of control.**
- **formalisation** and **standardisation.**

Organisational structures can be classified according to:

- how tasks are grouped together ie departmentalised - leads to specialisation.
- the degree of formalisation ie written rules, regulations, procedures, etc.
- the no. of layers in the hierarchy and width of the span of control.
- the extent to which authority and responsibility is shared (centralised v decentralised).

© APT Initiatives Ltd, 2009

Functional, Divisional and Matrix Structures – Potential Advantages and Disadvantages:

Functional:

Potential advantages – Such structures can…

- maximise efficiency - due to specialisation.
- minimise duplication - clearly defined roles.
- simplify training - jobs within one area.
- provide comfortable working atmosphere - people with same interests.

Potential disadvantages:

- Narrow perspective - staff focus on own area - lose sight of overall goal.
- Coordination across units difficult - diverse interests / perspectives.
- Limit experience - fail to develop top management generalists.

Regular communication between functions can minimise disadvantages.

Divisional: *Such structures can…*

- maximise efficiency - as a result of specialisation.
- lead to a better quality product / service to customers - as staff are more aware / able to respond quickly to changing customer needs.

Matrix:

Potential advantages:

- Lateral and vertical (upwards & downwards) communication - free flow of ideas - greater idea generation.
- More likely to identify potential problems / issues with an idea - as teams of people looking at project from different angles.
- Greater understanding and commitment to changes required to produce new products / enter new markets.

Potential disadvantages:

- Overlapping authority, thus one person only should be given full authority during the life of a project and this should be made clear to all concerned.
- More complex to manage - implications for management recruitment and training.

Formal, Mechanistic v Informal, Organic:

Mechanistic:

Potential advantages: Can…

- aid coordination, efficiency.
- reduce potential for conflict.
- minimise chance for error.

Potential disadvantages: May result in…

- demotivation, impersonal relationships.
- slow response to change.

Organic:

Such informal structures can:

- respond more quickly to the environment.
- aid motivation.

Factors Influencing Choice of Organisational Structure

Size

The larger the business, the more formal and complicated its structure.

As a business grows in size…

- supervisory / managerial layers develop to aid control / coordination.
- people tend to be grouped into separate departments that are allocated different tasks.
- written policies, rules, regulations are drawn up to coordinate and control member activities.

Environment

Examples:

- Dynamic - informal, organic, decentralised – able to respond quickly.
- Stable – less need for flexibility.
- Highly competitive – informal, organic – fast response.
- Low competition – less need for organic.
- Lots of stakeholders and / or variables – decentralised.

Nature of Tasks & Technology

Examples:

- Complicated technology, un-routine tasks – flexible, less formal structure.
- Less complex technology, routine tasks – formal, mechanistic.
- Wide product range, various locations – divisional rather than functional.
- Diverse, unrelated activities, geographically spread – decentralised.
- Much similarity between activities / operations – centralised - economies.

Corporate Objectives & Strategy

Examples:

- Differentiation strategy requires fast response to changing customer needs - less formal, flexible structure.
- Low cost strategy - more formal, mechanistic - to maximise efficiency.
- Aim to be market leader, first to bring out new products - flexible, organic structure.

Nature & Expectations of the Workforce

Example: Highly skilled, educated, professional workforce expect freedom, autonomy, dislike close supervision – more flexible, decentralised structure.

Beliefs & Preferences of Owners / Managers

Example: Autocratic owner / manager may insist on a formal structure and centralised decision making to ensure tight control over members' activities.

Closing Comments

Individuals have some control over structure. The continued growth of a business perhaps rests on the ability of the individuals who hold the power base to adopt the type of structure that best suits the business and its surrounding environment.

© **APT Initiatives Ltd**, 2009

Adapting Organisational Structures to Improve Competitiveness

Centralisation: the process of keeping the authority and responsibility for decision making in the upper levels of management.

Decentralisation: the process of passing authority and responsibility for decision making downwards from the upper levels of management to people at lower levels in the organisation.

Delayering: the removal of one or more managerial or supervisory layers.

Core and periphery workforce: refers to the use of a core of permanent, full-time workers and a periphery of temporary, part-time workers in order to provide the flexibility required to cope with variations in demand. The core workers generally fill important roles ie roles considered to be essential to the firm's competitive advantage, and tend to be more trained and skilled. The periphery workers may not be as skilled or well trained, or may be skilled workers brought in for a specific purpose.

Annual hours contracts: where employees are required to work a certain number of hours each year. The hours worked each week will vary throughout the year according to the needs of the business.

Zero hours contracts: where people are expected to be available for work as and when required. There are no set hours or times.

Outsourcing: the process of employing outside contractors to perform tasks which although are not core activities of the organisation, were previously performed in-house; or the act of moving a firm's internal activities and decision making responsibilities to outside providers.

The Importance of Structure:

Organisational structure can affect the:

- motivation of staff.
- efficiency, costs, profitability.
- speed of response to changes.

In an increasingly competitive market place one way to improve competitiveness is to adapt the organisational structure.

Centralisation and Decentralisation:

Appropriateness depends upon the:

- nature of the business and its activities.
- size and geographical spread of the business.
- environment in which the business operates.
- ability of employees.
- **risk** involved – the greater the risk, the more centralisation is likely.

A standardised approach (ie centralised or decentralised) may not be appropriate for **all** management functions, it depends upon **cost** and **efficiency.**

Centralisation:

Potential advantages:

- Greater control.
- Uniformity of decision making.
- Economies of scale.
- Economies of staffing.
- Economies of specialisation.

Potential disadvantages:

- Decisions might be too general.
- Overload / pressure on senior managers (MGR's).
- Too much power to senior MGR's.
- Slower decision making.
- Poor motivation of lower level staff.
- Loss of initiative of lower level staff.

Decentralisation:

Potential advantages:

- Reduced workload/stress of senior MGR's.
- Power is dispersed.
- Better quality decisions, MGR's.
- Faster decision making / response.
- Improved morale / motivation of lower level MGR's.
- Increased respect from staff.
- Lower supervision costs.

Potential disadvantages:

- Loss of direction and control.
- Lack of uniformity and consistency.
- Loss of economies of scale.
- Inter-unit conflict – narrow view.

Requirements: Managers to be capable of doing more / feel confident; trust.

Potential Problems:
Unwillingness to accept responsibility due to:

- feel extra responsibility without extra pay.
- lack of confidence.
- concern over greater accountability.

Overcoming barriers/changing attitudes:

Shorter-term: training, financial rewards. Long-term: adapt recruitment - select individuals happy with empowerment.

NB Feedback to the centre is still a necessary feature - to maintain effective control and assess whether the delegated authority is being used effectively.

Delayering:

Problems with tall structures:

- Poor and / or slow communication.
- Slower decision-making.
- Slower response to change.

The flatter, leaner the organisation, the fitter, more able to cope with a rapidly changing EVT.

Often used when business faces difficult times, and needs to cut costs in order to survive.

Delayering can:

- speed up communication, decisions.
- enable more rapid response.

Widens the span of control of lower level managers, which can:

- improve motivation, morale.
- lower supervision costs.

If too wide, however, it can over-burden managers and result in inefficiency.

Potential problems – delayering:

- often leads to **redundancies** - if staff cannot be redeployed, *which…*
- …increases costs - redundancy pay.
- …cause **ill feeling, lowers morale.**

Minimising the problems:

- Explain the reasoning behind the decision, staff consultation.

© **APT Initiatives Ltd**, 2009

Flexible Workforces:

Examples – Overview:

- Part-time (under 40hrs) instead of full-time eg am, pm, weekends, term time.
- Temporary (under 1 yr) not permanent.
- Flexitime, self-rostering, compressed working week.
- Annualised hours contracts.
- Zero hours contracts.
- Home working (teleworking).
- Outsourcing.

Potential Benefits for employee:

- Alleviates stress in balancing home life and work.

Potential Benefits for employer:

- Increases productivity, efficiency – not paying for labour not fully utilised.
- Helps to recruit staff more easily.
- Lower labour turnover & associated costs.

Annualised Hours:

Employees are required to work a certain no. of hours each year. Weekly hours vary according to business needs.

Zero Hours:

Employees are expected to be available for work as and when required. There are no set hours or times.

Core and Peripheral Workers:

Core – permanent, full-time: important roles, more trained, skilled, provide skills for competitive advantage and functional flexibility.

Peripheral – temporary, part-time: may not be as skilled or well trained, or skilled workers for specific purpose, provide numerical flexibility.

The use of part-time and temporary staff can increase a business's flexibility to meet fluctuations in demand and maximise capacity utilisation. *However,* it may be more costly than other methods to secure flexibility such as overtime, due to the extra recruitment, induction, training and admin involved (unless agency staff are used).

In addition, such staff may be less motivated and committed than permanent, full time staff.

Homeworking: This has arisen from developments in ITC. It is common to sales, accounting, proof-reading and editing jobs. *Cost benefits* – It can reduce…

- …fixed costs eg rent, rates.
- …travel expenses.
- …the need to invest in social facilities.

Other advantages: It can:

- have a positive effect on motivation as employees feel trusted (self esteem).
- alleviate stress as there is no commuting during the rush hour.
- be more productive as there are fewer interruptions and more time is spent working, less travelling.
- reduce air pollution!

However,

- There is the cost involved to provide the technology.
- It is more difficult to monitor working hours.
- It may result in worker isolation – with staff out of touch with business goals.
- The lack of social interaction may negatively affect motivation (social needs).
- It is, obviously, not possible on a full-time basis if the job requires direct contact with customers.

Outsourcing:

Assessing Appropriateness / Use:

Eg Outsourcing manufacture may be used:

- when a firm is not able to produce efficiently.
- when a firm lacks the specialist knowledge or equipment.
- when a firm is already operating at maximum capacity.
- to cope with seasonal demand.
- to cope with 'one-off' peaks in demand.

Potential Advantages:

- Cost reduction (particularly labour).
- Improved efficiency.
- Specialist expertise.
- Enhanced flexibility.
- Minimises inventory, materials handling.
- Allows focus on critical / core activities.

Potential Problems / Disadvantages:

- Depends on the availability of a lower cost firm.
- Quality of product, reliability of supply.
- Danger in being tied to an outside supplier.
- Protection of intellectual property.
- Involves a great deal of trust.
- Danger of information leaks.
- Less flexibility re: unexpected developments.
- Possible loss of control.
- Effect on workforce – redundancies.

Steps in Outsourcing Decisions:

1. Distinguish between core (competitive advantage) and non-core activities.
2. Be prepared to outsource non-core (**not core**) activities.
3. Identify possible providers.
4. Compare the cost with the in-house costs and non quantifiable factors eg quality.
5. If external firm can provide at lower price, same in-house quality, then proceed.
6. If no suitable provider found - keep the activity in-house, but continue the search!

Closing Comments re: Organisational Change

Implementing changes to the workplace is a sensitive issue. If not managed well it can create conflicts with staff and negatively affect performance. Businesses should, therefore, ensure that any changes:

- are fully discussed and agreed with employees and their representatives.
- comply with UK / EU legislation eg Working Time Directive, Sunday Trading.

© **APT Initiatives Ltd**, 2009

EFFECTIVE EMPLOYER / EMPLOYEE RELATIONS

Managing Communications with Employees

Communication: the process of transferring information between people. It involves messages being sent and received, with confirmation of receipt, and interpretation of the message, being returned by the receiver to the sender. Effective communication is, therefore, a two-way process where information is passed from person to person in spoken, written or visual form.

Formal communication: involves channels that have been approved by senior management and are officially recognised.

Informal communication: refers to information shared outside official channels.

Vertical communication: concerns information that flows from the upper hierarchical levels to the lower hierarchical levels (ie downwards communication) and vice versa (upwards communication).

Lateral (or horizontal) communication: communication that takes place across the organisation ie between people at the same level in the organisational hierarchy.

Diagonal communication: takes place when employees report to managers within different departments.

Communication networks: concern the way information flows between people in a particular work group.

Barriers to communication: are factors that prevent a message from being received and / or correctly understood or interpreted.

The Communication Process:

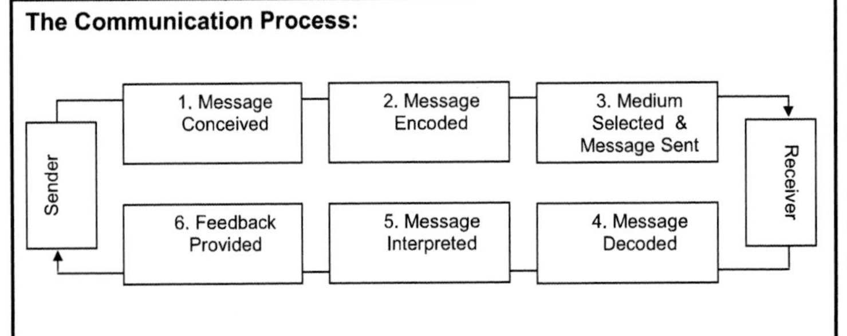

1. **Conceived.** S aware message to send, decides outline content.
2. **Encoded.** Message put into words, diagrams, body language, etc.
3. **Transmitted.** Via verbal eg written, oral; non-verbal eg body language, picture.
4. **Decoded.** R 'reads' message.
5. **Interpreted.** R deciphers meaning.
6. **Feedback.** R sends S confirmation received, interpreted, understood eg via email, nod, etc.

Importance:

Meeting customer / business needs – *It ensures:*

- employees clear on roles, tasks.
- MGT decisions carried through.
- potential problems identified, discussed at early stage - allowing timely action.

Motivating employees:

- Info on what needs to be done, how, by when - relieves anxiety (**safety** needs).
- Feedback on performance – important to satisfy **esteem** needs.
- Requires interaction of people – helps satisfy **social** needs.

Devising and implementing strategy:

- Customer research, feedback is vital to determine the most appropriate strategy.
- Employee feedback is vital in identifying problems at the implementation stage.
- Communicating the reasons / potential benefits can lessen potential resistance.

Types of Communication:

Communication can be classified according to:

- the **media** used - verbal (written, oral); non-verbal (image, illustration, body language)
- whether it is through **official or unofficial** channels - formal, informal.
- the **direction** in which info flows in relation to the hierarchy - vertical, lateral and diagonal.
- the **way** it flows between people in a **work group** - communication networks.

Verbal – Oral: *Eg's:* chat, interview, meeting - face to face, via video conference, telephone, Internet (Skype), loudspeaker.

Advantages:

- cheaper, direct.
- immediate exchange, instant feedback.
- opportunity for clarification.
- can expose attitudes.

Disadvantage:

- Without written / recorded record - points may be missed, forgotten - disputes.

Best used for:

- personal, important, unpleasant matters.

Effectiveness may depend upon:

- tone of voice, pitch, volume, speed and clarity of expression.

Verbal – Written: *Eg's:* memo, letter, report, email, text via notice board, post, computer / internet, fax, mobile phone.

Advantages:

- permanent record - revisited, checked.
- responses do not have to be immediate.
- time can be taken to read, 'digest' - ensure understand, develop response.

However:

- take time to produce.
- may be costly.
- less personal.
- open to misinterpretation.
- no immediate exchange.
- lots of paperwork – stressful.

Best used: to clarify oral, for complex matters, when staff can't receive the info at the same time.

Effectiveness may depend upon: vocabulary used, punctuation, grammar, clarity of expression.

© **APT Initiatives Ltd**, 2009

Non-verbal – Images / Illustrations: *Examples:* table, chart, graph, diagram, map, drawing, painting, photograph. *Use:* open meetings, training, conferences.

Advantages:

- reinforce written or oral.
- enable simplification of written, spoken.
- need fewer words.

However:

- open to wider misinterpretation.
- may take long time to prepare.

Non-verbal – Body Language:

Examples: facial expression, posture, gesture eg smile wagging finger, handshake. Can influence how messages are received and understood.

Vertical:

Downwards – used by MGT to give instructions, assign duties, responsibilities, provide general information.

Upwards – used by employees to provide feedback, make suggestions, seek clarification, air grievances.

Lateral:

Eg: R&D informing Finance of new product development costs.

Usually used to: share information and ideas, solve problems, resolve conflict.

Diagonal: *Occurs…*

- in projects that involve several departments and there are no clear lines of authority.
- where employees are required to report to two different managers.
- in matrix organisational structures.

Informal:

Outside official channels *eg member of staff:*

- seeking advice from someone other than his / her supervisor.
- passing on rumours to friends in other departments (ie via the grapevine).

Too much informal can:

- lower productivity.
- lead to the untimely release of confidential information

Too much informal can also lead to information getting distorted. *However, it is…*

- important in satisfying social needs.

It can also be used effectively by MGT to share information and, *for example to:*

- judge staff reaction to planned changes.
- make amendments before implementation to ensure acceptance.

Formal:

Set procedures re: language, medium - to maintain consistency, efficiency. *Eg:*

- Standard application form – recruitment.
- planned agenda – weekly meeting.
- purchase order – suppliers.

Communication Networks:

The Wheel

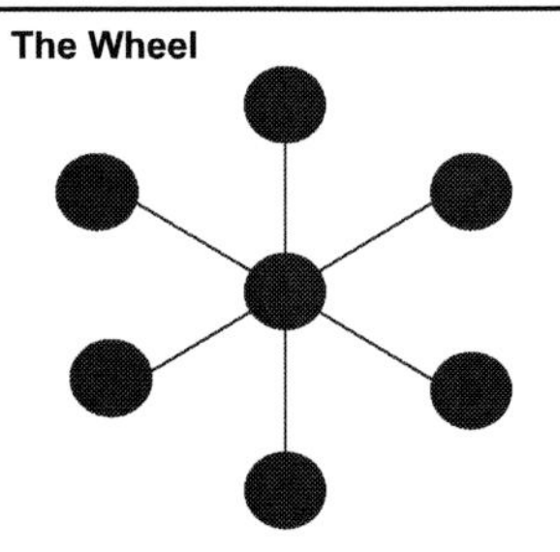

Communication to / from a central person, section, department – *Eg…*

- Department head briefing staff.
- Head office communicating price change to branch and receiving confirmation actioned.

Associated with:

- vertical communication.
- highly centralised organisations.

Advantages / Disadvantages:

- Fast, efficient *but…* only if not too many people are involved.
- No interaction.
- Person at centre has full control.
- Creativity may be stifled.

The Circle:

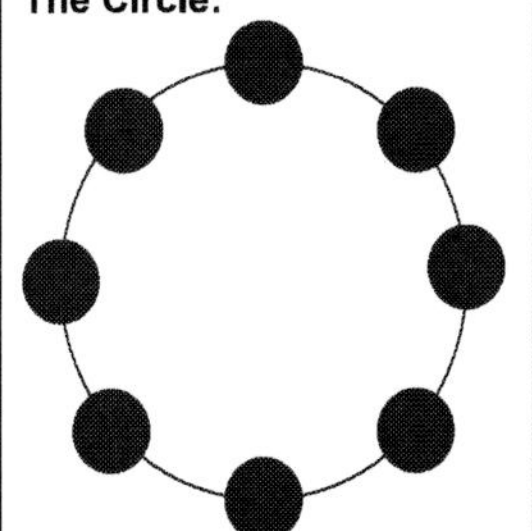

Individual people, sections or departments communicate with **two** other people, sections, departments.

Associated with: lateral communication.

Advantages / Disadvantages:

- More social interaction than wheel.
- Slow to pass on messages.
- Difficult to reach agreements - no-one to co-ordinate.
- Slower decision making.

The Chain:

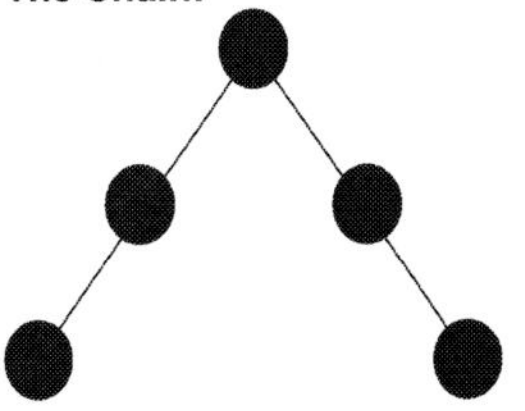

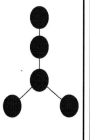

Information communicated by one individual, section, department, who then passes it on to someone else. *Example:* In a formal organisational hierarchy - senior management through middle to junior management.

Advantages / Disadvantages:

- Isolation - person at bottom.
- Slow decision making - intermediaries involved.

All-channel:

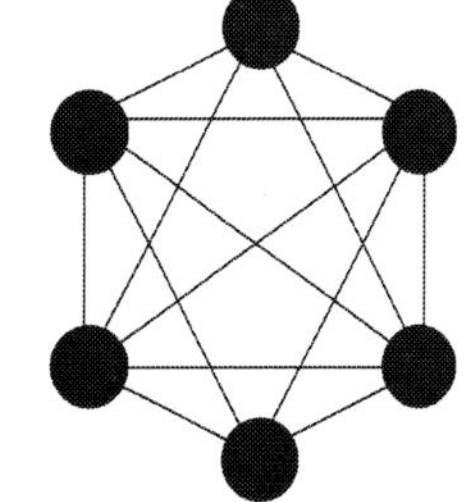

No central figure - each person communicates with anyone. Only possible with small groups. Common to decentralised organisations.

Advantages / Disadvantages:

- Creativity - lots of interaction.
- Conflict and slow decision making.

© **APT Initiatives Ltd**, 2009

Barriers to Effective Communication:

Intermediaries:

Too many could lead to: long delays, message getting distorted, message never being passed on. Latter occurs accidentally, or deliberately, when there is:

- a power struggle / clash between sender / receiver.
- nervousness, embarrassment, resentment, bias.
- uncertainty over accuracy - lack of understanding.
- lack of open-mindedness.
- fear of difficult reaction.
- intermediaries - not seeing message as important.

Above often happens as a business increases in size - when management / supervisory levels develop to:

- control use of organisational resources.
- maximise productivity and efficiency .

But… the greater the number of levels:

- the greater the opportunity for information to get distorted/lost - creates conflict/operational problems
- the longer it takes for the process to take place, resulting in slower decision making.

Possible solution – Decentralisation:

- Speeds up communication / decision-making processes.
- Reduces communication overload, stress on managers.

Overload:

The link with size: Large firms - lots of information given out and gathered - to ensure consistency and control.

Too much paperwork may lead to:

- difficulty finding documentation when required.
- difficulty prioritising.
- key information being missed - limited time to respond.
- failure to respond to urgent requests.

Ultimately:

- Receiver feeling stressed leading to low productivity, absenteeism and associated costs.

The link with IT:

- Easier and quicker to generate and send large amounts of data – receiver unable to process all the information.

Lack of Common Sense of Purpose:

If receiver feels:

- excessive use of jargon.
- alienated.
- not committed to the achievement of organisational goals.
- personal goals conflict with those of the sender.
- no 'common sense of purpose'.

Then:

- unlikely to be willing to receive / listen to new ideas.
- may listen but not give message full attention.
- may lack interest in the subject matter.
- may believe it bears little relevance to him / her.

Lack of Common Language:

Decoding problems can arise when there is:

- excessive use of jargon.
- sentence structure, general English - different to the receiver.
- over-simplified language that the receiver finds condescending.

Result: message not acted upon - inadequate feedback.

Attitudes:

A mental view / opinion held by an individual or group which influences their behaviour. Concerns: likes / dislikes.

Personality conflicts help or hinder communication.

Examples:

Sender dislikes receiver, then may:

- make it deliberately difficult for message to be understood.
- use sarcasm, innuendo, over simplified language.

Can cause resentment and lead to message being:

- completely ignored.
- incorrectly acted upon.
- receiver reading what he / she expects, not what is actually there.

Receiver dislikes the sender, then may:

- make less effort to decode message / understand.
- deliberately misinterpret message.
- deliberately limit feedback.

Receiver who dislikes subject of the message may:

- be unwilling to listen to the message.
- fail to act upon it.

Low Morale:

The mental or emotional condition of an individual or group of individuals.

Sender – may not take the time to:

- compose the message carefully - resulting in vagueness, ambiguity.
- consider receiver's abilities/limits – resulting in inappropriate language – problems in understanding.
- select an appropriate medium.

Receiver – may:

- ignore message.
- easily get sidetracked, distracted.
- not take the time to understand.
- not take the time to interpret it correctly.
- deliberately misinterpret it.
- fail to provide feedback.

Environment: Concerns the place where the message is transmitted.

Concentration may be affected by a…

- hot stuffy atmosphere or inadequate heating resulting in discomfort.
- noisy workplace eg factory or busy office - hinders hearing.
- lack of privacy - may cause embarrassment, distraction.

Time:

Concerns the time of day, length of communication, how long the sender / receiver have available.

Choosing the right time, right place is important, because:

- If rushed - important points get missed.
- If late - too tired - unable to 'digest' new information.
- If document / conversation lengthy - hard to concentrate - points missed.

Position / Status:

- Communication with a superior is generally more formal, restrained – employee may not be honest when consulted.
- Older employee may resent taking orders from young, newly appointed supervisor.

© **APT Initiatives Ltd**, 2009

Ensuring Effective Communication:

1. Think carefully before communicating.
2. Be direct, honest, prepared to listen.
3. Consider time factors.
4. Select an appropriate environment eg with ample:
   - space.
   - seating.
   - ventilation.
5. Choose the most appropriate method and style of communication eg taking into account the:
   - aim of the communication.
   - relationship with the receiver.
   - attitudes to the subject under discussion.
   - knowledge / ability of the receiver.
   - nature of the message.
6. Be aware of physical responses eg those that convey:
   - interest and enthusiasm.
   - impatience.
   - boredom.
   - arrogance.
   - nervousness.

The Use of IT:

Can speed up communication, decisions.

Costs:

- Initial capital, installation, training.
- running costs.

But can reduce costs in longer-term - eg:

- email - save printing, stationery, postage.
- video-conferencing - save on travel.

Potential problems:

- mechanical faults, breakdowns.
- information overload.
- security, confidentiality.
- non-business use - productivity.
- employee resistance to new methods.

NB The AQA specification focuses on the importance of effective communication for employee / employer relations. Communication is, however, also essential in maintaining effective relationships with external stakeholders eg suppliers, customers, potential investors, and ensuring a positive public image.

Methods of Employee Representation

Employee representation: involves providing workers with the opportunity to air their views on work related matters. It may take many forms including representation through trade union officials and the process of collective bargaining, works councils who meet regularly, or other ad hoc groups.

Consultation: where managers ask employees their views on work related matters, either directly or through representatives, before a decision is made.

Works council: where employee representatives form a permanent committee with the right to discuss / influence work related decisions, usually excluding pay and other terms and conditions of employment.

Trade union: an organisation of workers created to protect and advance the interests of its members by negotiating agreements on pay and conditions of work.

Collective bargaining: a process whereby the employer negotiates with employee representatives, usually one or more trade unions, who act on behalf of their members to get improvements on pay, and other terms and conditions of employment.

The Legal Requirement for Representation:

Employees have a statutory right to be accompanied by a fellow worker or trade union official at disciplinary, grievance hearings.

Employers are legally required to consult employees over:

- planned collective redundancies.
- health & safety.

Employers may also have to inform and consult staff on other work related changes.

General Advantages and Disadvantages:

Disadvantages:

- Slower decision making.
- Greater scope for conflict.

Advantages:

- Employees feel valued, more fulfilled.
- More positive relationships with MGT.
- Early resolution of conflict.
- Easier implementation of decisions.
- Better quality decisions.

Trade Unions:

In firms with 21 or more staff, workers are allowed to vote on trade union recognition. A vote of 40% or more results in the relevant trade union(s) being recognised to negotiate with employers on behalf of the workforce on pay and other conditions (TU & LRC Act 1992).

TU Objectives - obtain the following for members:

- good rates of pay.
- good working conditions.
- job security.
- influence over government policy.

Main functions in terms of representation:

1. Individual representation.
2. Negotiation – collective bargaining.

© **APT Initiatives Ltd**, 2009

Trade Unions and Collective Bargaining:

For the **employee** being a member of a TU provides greater influence when negotiating.

For the **employer** – in the past union activity resulted in:

- increased labour costs.
- inflexible working practices.
- excessive disruptions (lost orders / sales).
- difficulties implementing change.

However, legislation in the 1980's greatly restricted union power, and collective bargaining through unions can actually result in:

- simpler, quicker negotiations.
- more realistic demands.
- support in implementing agreements.
- expertise in solving problems.
- improved morale, motivation, performance.
- compliance with legislation - lower costs.

The power of a trade union depends on union density - the proportion of workers who are members. It is calculated as a percentage:

$$\frac{\text{Number of workers who are members}}{\text{Total number of workers employed}} \times 100$$

The higher the %, the higher the density and greater the influence.

Works Councils:

In Europe, (under the TICER 1999) – works councils must be set up in firms that employ at least:

1. 1,000 workers in Europe.
2. 150 in each of at least two member states.

Membership:

- 3 to 30.
- at least one representative from each country.
- Management representatives.

Discuss, negotiate range of issues – *eg:*

- business performance.
- growth and development plans.
- changes in working practices.
- collective redundancies.

Can:

- develop positive relationships between management and staff - removal of 'them and us' attitudes.
- increase staff awareness and appreciation of factors influencing MGT decisions (and vice versa), *thus…*
- help employees (and managers) to be more 'reasonable' with their demands / expectations.

Other Forms of Representation: Worker directors, Quality circles, Employee shareholders.

Methods of Avoiding and Resolving Industrial Disputes

No strike deals: agreements formed between employee and management representatives not to strike in return for something eg higher wages, improved working conditions, limited redundancies.

Single union agreements: agreements between employee and management representatives to recognise and negotiate pay and other terms and conditions of employment with one single union covering the whole of the workforce.

Arbitration: where an independent person or panel listens to both sides of a dispute and decides the outcome.

Pendulum arbitration: where an independent person or panel listens to both sides of a dispute and chooses between the two sides rather than tries to form a compromise between the two.

Conciliation: the act of bringing together the parties in a dispute and helping them to reach a mutually agreeable solution.

Mediation: where an independent person or panel acts as an intermediary in talking and making suggestions to both sides but the final outcome is left for the parties to decide.

Industrial tribunal: a body of people set up to settle disputes between employers and employees, usually consisting of a legally qualified chairperson and two lay persons who decide the outcome of the dispute.

ACAS: the advisory, conciliation and arbitration service set up in 1975 to help prevent and settle industrial disputes.

Overview:

Sources of conflict:

- Rates of pay including overtime.
- Hours, breaks, holidays.
- Flexible working.
- New technology - different work tasks, groups, redundancies.

Resolved through:

- industrial action; use of intermediaries.

Reduced / eliminated by:

- single union or no strike agreements.

Types of Industrial Action:

Employees':

Organised action includes:

- Work to rule, Go slow, Overtime ban, Sit-ins, Work-ins, Strikes, Picketing.

Less noticeable, unorganised action:

- Lower work effort, lateness, absence.

Employers':

- Withdrawal of overtime & suspension.
- Lockouts.
- Changing standards & piecework rates
- Closure.

Consequences:

For the ***Employer:***

- Lost production.
- Unfulfilled orders.
- Lost revenue, profit.
- Cash flow problems.
- Loss of reputation, future custom.
- Lower morale, labour turnover, difficulties recruiting.

For the ***Employee:***

- Loss of earnings.

© **APT Initiatives Ltd**, 2009

Methods for Avoiding Conflict:

No Strike Deals: agreements not to strike in return for something eg higher wages, improved working conditions, limited redundancies, etc.

Single Union Agreements: one union covering whole of workforce is recognised and negotiated with on pay and other terms and conditions - to reduce time, complexity, conflict, admin involved in dealing with several unions.

Methods for Resolving Conflict:

Conciliation: 3rd party listens to both sides and encourages them to look for common ground and to reconcile their differences. No power to impose / recommend settlement. Tries to enable parties to reach their own agreement.

Arbitration: Independent person / panel listens to both sides and decides the outcome. Arbitrator's decision may or may not be legally binding. If both sides agree in advance, then the decision can be binding. If not, either side can reject the decision.

Pendulum Arbitration: Independent person / panel listens to both sides and chooses between the two, rather than trying to form a compromise. One side loses out completely. This encourages both to act reasonably and to try to get as close an agreement they can before taking it to pendulum arbitration.

Mediation: Independent person / panel acts as an intermediary in talking and making suggestions to both sides, but the final outcome is left for the parties to decide. Differs from conciliation as the mediator makes suggestions.

Industrial Tribunal: A body of people set up to settle disputes between employers and employees. Usually a legally qualified chairperson and 2 lay persons who decide the outcome of the dispute. Where an employer is found to be at fault the tribunal can insist the employee is awarded compensation or, in case of unfair dismissal, the employee is reinstated. Tribunal does not have the power to enforce their decision. This requires separate application to court.

The Role of ACAS:

Organisation:

Chairperson (full-time). Up to 15 members appointed by the Secretary of State for 5 yrs.

- One third after consultation with the TUC.
- One third after consultation with the CBI.
- The remaining are 'independents'.

ACAS has over 600 employees in regional offices in England, Wales and Scotland.

Role & Function re: disputes / resolving conflict:

- provide impartial, confidential information and advice over TU disputes.
- help resolve disputes over TU recognition by voluntary means.
- help resolve disputes when TU makes a claim for recognition under the ERA 1999.
- assist with membership checks and ballots to help resolve TU recognition.
- assist employers and TU to draw up recognition and procedural agreements, and work together to solve problems.

Also provides general advice including codes of practice to employees, TU's and employers, over a wide range of employment matters, eg employment legislation, workforce planning, recruitment, health & safety.

(Source: ACAS)

MAXIMISING YOUR PERFORMANCE IN THE EXAMINATION

© APT Initiatives Ltd, 2009

Summary of AQA GCE (AS/A2) Level Business Studies Mark Schemes

All GCE (AS/A2) Level Business Studies examinations test your ability to **use** your knowledge. The better you are at **using** your knowledge, the higher the mark awarded.

There are essentially 4 main skills an examiner looks for when deciding what marks to award you in your responses to examination questions. These consist of: **Knowledge, Application of knowledge, Analysis** and **Evaluation.** These skills can be ranked in ascending order of difficulty – knowledge being the easiest skill to demonstrate, and evaluation the hardest. As you progress through your course, greater emphasis is placed on the demonstration of evaluation skills. It is not possible to evaluate, analyse or apply knowledge, however, without first having acquired knowledge. Consequently, knowledge is the foundation of all your answers.

In general, you need to be able to demonstrate **all four skills** in order to secure high marks. These four levels of ability are the four main assessment objectives (AO's) of AQA GCE (AS/A2) Level Business Studies, and demonstration of knowledge and / or understanding without any application, analysis or evaluation is known as **'Content'** (AO1).

When the examiner reads your answer he / she actually looks for **evidence of each of the above skills / assessment objectives** and makes decisions about how well you have demonstrated each of these skills. For each assessment objective the examiner then **awards a mark depending upon the extent to which he / she feels each assessment objective has been demonstrated.** The diagram adjacent relating to a question worth 18 marks should help you understand the above points more clearly.

	Content 4 marks	Application 4 marks	Analysis 5 marks	*Evaluation 5 marks
Level 4	**4 marks** Candidate identifies two or more relevant points **and** shows good understanding			
Level 3	**3 marks** Candidate identifies two or more relevant points **and** shows limited understanding **or** one relevant point **and** limited understanding		**5 marks** Candidate shows strong, sustained analysis, developing points fully	**5 marks** Candidate shows good judgement, with full justification
Level 2	**2 marks** Candidate identifies two relevant points **or** shows good understanding **or** elements of both ie one relevant point **and** limited understanding	**4-3 marks** Candidate applies knowledge effectively	**4-3 marks** Candidate shows good analysis, with some effective development	**4-3 marks** Candidate shows some judgement, with some justification
Level 1	**1 mark** Candidate identifies one relevant point **or** shows limited understanding	**2-1 marks** Candidate attempts to apply knowledge	**2-1 marks** Candidate shows limited analysis, with little or no development	**2-1 mark** Candidate shows limited judgement, with little or no justification

*Marks awarded for 'Evaluation' are also based on the quality of your written communication.

The matrix shows that if a question is worth 18 marks and you only demonstrate content <u>and</u> application with no analysis or evaluation, then you can gain between 2 marks (1 for content + 1 for application) and 8 marks. The exact mark gained depends upon the extent to which you demonstrate each of these skills. NB Failure to demonstrate any of the above skills <u>in relation to the question set</u>, will gain zero marks. Let us now explore in-depth what you need to do to demonstrate each of the four skills.

Individual Assessment Objectives Explained

Content (AO1)

Content requires you to know or understand something relating to the question. Demonstrating this assessment objective may include:

- **providing a definition of a key business term;**
- **describing a theory or part of a theory;**
- **providing an example;**
- **providing a simple explanation of the facts, without referring to specific evidence presented in the case study or data response material.**

For example, in a question asking you to evaluate the use of delayering as a strategy to improve a particular business's competitiveness, defining what delayering is (ie the removal of supervisory or managerial layers in the organisational structure) and / or the costs and benefits associated with such a strategy **in general** (eg improved communication, faster decision making), demonstrates content.

Demonstration of knowledge and understanding on its own will not enable you to achieve a pass.

Application of Knowledge (AO2)

The ability to apply knowledge requires you to understand and appreciate the importance or significance of it, within the context provided for you in the question or case study. Demonstrating application of knowledge involves:

- **developing points thoroughly with specific reference to evidence presented in the case study / data response material.**

Following on from the delayering question above, to secure marks for application you would have to explain ***why*** delayering might be appropriate **for the particular business in question**. Let us assume, for example, that the case study informs us that the business in question designs, manufactures and markets computer games. Stating the following would secure marks for application… *'Because this business designs, manufacturers and markets its own products, delayering may help to reduce the time taken between a new idea being generated, discussed and approved for production, and production of the new product actually commencing'.*

NB Naming the business is not application; if the name can be replaced with another, without any change to the meaning of the answer, application has not been demonstrated.

Demonstration of application of knowledge and content only, will not earn higher than a D grade, and more likely a grade E.

© **APT Initiatives Ltd**, 2009

Analysis (AO3)

Analysis is about recognising and discussing relationships between different pieces of evidence and the possible causes or consequences of a particular aspect relating to the business or situation under review, by referring to some or all the evidence available. For example, it may involve acknowledging the challenges and risks associated with a proposal, or recognising the impact of a strategy on different stakeholders and their likely reaction to it. Any appropriate use of numerical data to develop understanding will also secure marks for analysis.

You cannot analyse (or evaluate) without first acquiring knowledge and understanding. If, for example, you were asked to evaluate the extent to which the case study business's success in achieving its objectives was dependent upon the production and implementation of a comprehensive marketing plan, you would first need to know what a marketing plan is, what they contain, and why they are important in general, before you can answer the question.

To demonstrate analysis, you must **ensure that every point made is considered and explored in detail, including the possible impact on the business and consequences for the business of any problems or issues being considered, and / or solutions you are putting forward.** Depending precisely on how a question is phrased, you have opportunities to present negative and positive impacts and consequences, both in the short term and long term, and with regard to a business's various stakeholders. Marks for analysis are, in fact, often awarded for considering **more than one point of view.** However, simply listing advantages and disadvantages if already obvious from the case study, will not secure marks for analysis. Your answers must **always go beyond what is already evident in the data you have been given to answer the question.** You must be **selective** and explain *why* something may be advantageous or disadvantageous for the case study business by taking into account, for example, the aims and objectives and influence and / or experience of the owners, shareholders and managers, as well as the business's markets, customers, suppliers, creditors, resources and economic climate, etc.

With reference to the question on delayering above, analysis would involve discussing ***why*** it may or may not help to improve the competitiveness of **this particular business** by considering the **impact** and the **consequences for this particular business**, always referring to any evidence provided about the business. For example, let us assume that the case study also informs us that the business in question has always struggled to be competitive on price, and that many of the managerial staff, who are being made redundant as a result of the delayering, have been employed by the business for over five years. You might, therefore, explain that... *'Labour costs would initially increase as the majority of staff involved would be entitled to redundancy pay. However, in the longer term, delayering would help to reduce labour costs and with lower costs the business would be able to reduce prices, thereby making it more competitive'.*

The above answer - in just two sentences - demonstrates analysis (and application). It makes **good use of the information provided** in the case study to consider the **impact** and **consequences** of delayering for **the particular business in question** and **in the context provided,** ie as a means to improve the business's competitiveness.

Consistently demonstrating analysis, with some application of knowledge and content, is likely to secure a B and, possibly, an A grade.

Evaluation (AO4):

Evaluation concerns actually **judging** which solutions you put forward are the best, or points you have made are the most relevant or significant, based exclusively on what has been analysed. Evaluation may be achieved by:

- **prioritising points / suggestions**, for example, by ranking them in time order, stating what should be done in the short term, and what in the long term, with reasons why;
- **assessing the extent to which your suggestions will work** and explaining **on what success any proposals you put forward may be based;**
- **assessing the degree of impact** based on alternative solutions.

All decisions should be **logical** and **balanced**. To ensure they are you need to:

- **consider all the evidence presented** in the case study and **more than one side to an argument.** There is often no 'one best way' and answers should recognise that there are a variety of responses to any situation and discuss all the alternatives.

- **explain the reasons behind preferred options** which must be **related to evidence presented** in the question. With regards to this, the **suitability** and **feasibility** of any of your proposals should take into account the following:

  - the nature of the business, its markets and activities;
  - the aims and objectives of the business;
  - its resources;
  - the objectives, power and activities of other key stakeholders, in particular, customers, competitors and owners / shareholders;
  - government policy and the economic climate;
  - other external influences such as legislation.

A key point to recognise and emphasise with regard to evaluation is that information presented is often one-sided ie biased. Therefore, you must **look out for and be able to distinguish between fact and opinion.** Evidence which comes from an unreliable source, or is somewhat out of date should also be recognised in your judgements. Furthermore, all the information required to form a definitive conclusion, is not always provided in the case study / data response material. Therefore,

- **identifying what information is missing and explaining *why* it might be required, *how* it might be used, or *how* it might affect the assessment of a particular problem / issue / situation, or decision to be made, will demonstrate evaluation.**

Overall, you will need to make decisions between conflicting arguments, put forward your opinion based on case study evidence, and justify your selection by weighing up the advantages and disadvantages of each alternative.

© **APT Initiatives Ltd**, 2009

Key Words & Phrases to Build 'Higher Level' Answers

AO2: Application of Knowledge & Understanding

- In this case…
- This means that…
- Because…

AO3: Analysis

- Therefore…
- This will lead to…
- The effect of this is…
- This is likely to result in…
- However…
- On the other hand…
- The dis / advantages of this are…
- The consequences of this are…
- The impact of this is…
- If X happens then Y might occur, if A happens then B might occur

AO4: Evaluation

- Overall…
- On balance…
- In the short-term / long-term…
- The most likely cause is… because…
- The greatest effect that this will have on the business is… because…
- The most appropriate solution out of those discussed is… because…
- In these circumstances it is more likely / less likely that… because…
- This may be more / less important when… because…
- Whether this leads to… depends upon…
- Whether this works depends upon…
- The extent of the impact of this issue will depend upon…

Additional Phrases to Use in the Examination

Never be certain. There is often evidence missing and a range of external factors influencing the situation or business presented in the question that could change at any time, and influence the outcome. Therefore,

- avoid stating will, must, should, would, ought to, have to.
- use other less definite words and phrases such as **may, might, could,** and **it is possible that.**

Command Words & Appropriate Responses

At A2 level Business Studies you are only likely to be asked questions that provide scope for analytical or evaluative responses (ie AO3 and AO4). Not all questions provide scope for, or require, evaluative answers. It is important to be aware of the sort of answer the examiner is seeking. An obvious indicator is the number of marks allocated for a question (or part question). The other key indicator is the first few words or the 'command' word or phrase used in the question. Hence, the table below outlines the type of response required by the various command words or phrases that might be used in AQA GCE A2 Level questions. The assessment objective required (ie AO3 and AO4) has also been identified. Knowledge of these will help to ensure that you do not over-run on questions not requiring evaluative answers, and preserve time for those that do.

QUESTIONS	RESPONSE	AO
Analyse	Consider all viewpoints, describe their inter-relationship	3
Assess	Judge how important or successful something is	4
Comment upon	Give a point of view; decide how true something is	4
Consider	Take into account the advantages and disadvantages and form an opinion about something	4
Discuss	Describe different aspects of the subject / present two sides of the argument and give a reasoned conclusion	4
Evaluate	Examine different sides to the question and try to reach a conclusion; judge the worth / value of	4
Examine	Consider in depth; make a point and fully develop it	3
Explain why	Make clear and give reasons for	3
How / why might	Present and evaluate evidence for and against	3
Justify	Give reasons to support an argument or action	4
Recommend	Consider the evidence and make a judgement supporting a particular course of action	4
To what extent	Determine how true something is, by explaining both sides to an argument and evaluating / making a judgement	4

The Structure of the Paper

Unit 3 is marked out of **80.** You have **1 hour** and **45 minutes** to answer the questions. All the questions are compulsory and require extended answers based on an unseen case study.

You need to take care not to spend too much time on the question worth the least marks and leave yourself short of time to complete questions requiring more extended responses, carrying high marks. Allowing for time to read through the paper and to read through your answers at the end (to check for any errors or omissions including any grammatical errors) you have approximately **90 minutes** to answer all the questions. This equates to just over **1 minute per mark**. Therefore, for questions worth 10 marks (eg Analyse…) you should not take longer than 12 minutes to write your answer. For questions worth 18 marks (eg To what extent…), you should try to write your answer within 20 minutes, and for questions worth 34 marks (eg those requiring you to analyse two options and make a justified recommendation) you should try to write your answer in under 40 minutes.

Practicing doing questions in a set time limit is **absolutely essential.** Many students have the knowledge and ability to secure high grades but fail due to lack of time.

NB The structure and requirements of examination papers may change from time to time, and so it is important to check that the above information still applies since the publication of this book.

© **APT Initiatives Ltd**, 2009

TOP TIPS TO MAXIMISE YOUR PERFORMANCE IN THE EXAMINATION

1. **Read** through the **entire question paper** at least **twice**.

2. Work out **approximate timings** for each question. This should be based on the number of marks per question and the total time allowed. With questions worth 18 or more marks, you must allow a few minutes to plan. **Planning** will help to keep your answers to the point, logical, and will help you to prioritise – all essential to secure high grades.

3. Answer the question you find the **easiest first.** This will help to build up your confidence.

4. **Read the question carefully.** Make sure you fully understand what you are being asked to do **before** you start writing.

5. For questions involving **calculations always show your workings out.** Marks can be gained for using the correct formula / method of approach if the final answer is incorrect.

6. Treat every answer as discrete / self-contained ie **do not refer the examiner back to points you have made in previous answers.** (This is especially relevant with the advent of on-line marking).

7. **Keep within the time allowed.** If you start to run over time on one question, stop and come back to it at the end. (Students often gain the most marks in the first part of their answer).

8. **Regularly read through your work** not just at the end. Firstly, to check all points make sense and directly relate to the question set. (Many students, once they start writing, stray from the original question and this wastes valuable time). Secondly, to check for spelling, punctuation and grammatical areas – marks are awarded for quality of written communication.

9. If you think you've missed an important point out – **don't panic!** Mark where you want to make this point and direct the examiner to a relevant section at the end.

For questions carrying high marks:

10. Think about your answer and, where relevant, your **conclusion**, **<u>before</u>** you start writing.

11. **Brainstorm** the **relevant points** and write these down in rough in the form of a spider diagram. Write these directly on your question paper. The examiner will review any rough notes made if you run out of time.

12. **Prioritise** the order in which the above points will be discussed. Write a number next to each point in the order that you intend to discuss them.

13. **Introduce** your answer – explain how you intend to answer the question, show that you have understood the question.

14. Discuss **more than one point** in depth, consider **more than one side** to an argument.

15. Keep **referring back** to the original question set <u>and</u> the case study business **<u>throughout</u>** your answer.

16. Consider the possible **advantages** or **disadvantages** and / or the **implications / impact / effect** of any problems, issues or solutions being considered on the case study business – always referring to evidence presented in the case study.

17. Always try to **conclude** each question – What do you consider to be the **most important, significant, relevant** point your have made and ***why*** is it for **this particular business?** What should be done in the <u>short term</u>? <u>long term</u>? *<u>Why</u>?* Consider the **objectives** of the case study business, the **resources** available <u>and</u> the **likelihood of success** (taking into account the strengths and weaknesses of the business, and opportunities and threats), as applicable.

18. **Have <u>CONFIDENCE in YOURSELF</u> –** you now have a great deal of knowledge. ***<u>Use</u>* this knowledge well!**

© **APT Initiatives Ltd**, 2009